ACADEMY OF
LEARNING

Your Complete Preschool Lesson Plan Resource: Volume 6

© 2015 Breely, Crush & Associates, LLC

Ver. 112214

Table of Contents

Educator Biography

Sharlit Elliott has a B.S. in Elementary Education and Early Childhood from Brigham Young University and has been a teacher for over 15 years working with children ages 3-5. She keeps current on changes in education by attending University classes and conferences several times a year. Besides having raised five children, she has held various leadership positions with the Girl Scouts and the 4-H program. She enjoys gardening, scrapbooking, reading and of course working with children.

How to Use This Book

This book is designed for a teacher working with children ages 3-5 in a classroom, homeschool or home preschool environment. One of the most important aspects of this series is that it includes fun activities that will enhance their skills. These lessons plans, games and ideas are all for you to use. Don't forget, these are complete lessons and activities that have been designed for compliance with federal and state guidelines for education. We go above and beyond to bring you MORE than what's expected in the public school system.

We will refer to your students as "your children or class". That includes whatever area you are using these lessons for: homeschool or preschool. Our lesson plans include improving student's abilities through activities. The skills we will be working with include: listening skills, music, movement, language and literacy, mathematics, science, fine motor, creative art, sensory, dramatic play, and social skills.

The book is organized by themes which will help you quickly find just the right information. The headings in the book will direct you quickly to large group, small group, and free time activities. It will also provide ideas for field trips.

This book will include the following areas:

Group Activities/Circle Time

- Music & Movement is used to help develop large muscles in arms and legs. These need to be developed before children can be successful in small muscles activities such as used in writing or cutting with scissors. This area also helps children learn to enjoy music and the basics such as beat, loud/soft and fast/slow.

- Language & Literacy is how we help children learn vocabulary, story order, thinking skills, recall, concepts of the theme, and expressive language.

Small Group Activities/Table Times

- Math & Cognitive is used to teach numbers, shapes, patterns, sorting, thinking and reasoning skills.

- Fine Motor Skills develop small muscles to be able to draw, write, manipulate small things, to tear, and to cut with scissors.

- Language & Literacy is used to develop skills such as expressive writing, visual memory, matching letters, letter sounds, categorizing items, directional words, and opposites.

- Other creative activities to develop their own uniqueness as an individual.

Free Time

- Creative arts to draw, build, and develop their imagination.

- Sensory activities are used to learn through exploration and using their senses.

- Dramatic Play & Social Development let children take on different roles, solve problems, find solutions, and develop social interactions.

- Science helps children explore by experimenting, identifying problems, guessing what will happen, checking to see what did happen, questioning how things happened, and developing a plan of what to do next.

- Gross Motor Skills to practice using large and small muscles in fun activities.

- Field Trip Ideas to help children use real places to learn about the world.

Throughout the book we will use the following icons to show the different types of activities:

MUSIC & MOVEMENT

LANGUAGE & LITERACY

MATH & COGNITIVE

FINE MOTOR SKILLS

CREATIVE ARTS

SENSORY

DRAMATIC PLAY & SOCIAL DEVELOPMENT

SCIENCE

GROSS MOTOR SKILLS

FIELD TRIP IDEAS

Under the Sea

GROUP ACTIVITIES/CIRCLE TIME

MUSIC AND MOVEMENT

The first song to use is "Down by the Bay" from "Singable Songs for the Very Young" tape or CD by Raffi. Children love to sing the silly rhyming words to this song. Draw simple pictures that illustrate the rhyming words on card stock and put them in sequence of the song. Once they have learned these verses, have the children make up additional verses of rhyming words. Then, have the children draw pictures that represent the rhyming words.

"Baby Beluga" from "Baby Beluga" tape or CD by Raffi. Raffi also has a book by this same title with beautiful illustrations of the scenes in this song. Show the pictures of the book while playing the song the first time it is introduced. It makes the song come alive to students who may not have seen pictures of sea animals.

"Water Dance" from "Baby Beluga" tape or CD by Raffi. This music is an instrumental song in which Raffi provides music that sounds like a gentle stream that bursts into dance.

"Five Little Fish" from "Macmillan Sing & Learn Program" by Newbridge Communication Inc., on CD or tape. Have children hold up fingers to represent the number of fish swimming in the sea as the song progresses. They can also move their bodies to the swimming music.

One, Two, Three, Four, Five Once I Caught a Fish Alive – Author Unknown

One, two, three, four, five,

Once I caught a fish alive,

Six, seven, eight, nine, ten,

Then I let it go again.

Why did you let it go?

Because it bit my finger so.

Which finger did it bite?

This little finger on my right.

You could have the children pretend to row a boat while singing the following song.

Michael Row – Traditional Song

Mi-chael row the boat a-shore,

Hal-le-lu-jah,

Michael row the boat a-shore,

Hal-le-lu-jah

Repeat

Row, Row, Row Your Boat – Traditional Song

Row, row, row your boat,

Gently down the stream.

Merrily, merrily, merrily, merrily

Life is but a dream.

You can use the same melody and have the children think up different words to it. The new words may put a different emphasis on different things. The following is an example.

Fish, fish, fish with a pole,

Fish the sea today.

Pull them up, pull them up,

Each and every day.

"I Wish I Were a Fish" from "I Have A Song For You About Animals" tape and/or song book by Janeen Brady, Brite-Music Enterprises, Inc. Children have fun dancing around the room like fish.

"Seahorse Merry-Go-Round" from "I Have A Song For You About Animals" tape and/or song book by Janeen Brady, Brite-Music Enterprises Inc. Show pictures and talk about seahorses before singing this song. Explain that seahorses move up and down to get around. Have the children listen to the song and move like a seahorse up and down and around in a circle.

"Octopus's Garden" from "Five Little Monkeys" by Richard Starkey, Starkey Music Limited.

"My Very Own Octopus" by Bernard Most.

"Octopus" from "10 Carrot Diamond" CD by Charlotte Diamond. This is a fun song that has a good beat with lots of repetition. Children use their hands and arms to show the sea animal sizes by stretching them out wider and wider. They also use their fingers and arms to open the fish mouth to eat smaller fish than they are.

"Going Over the Sea" from "Just For Fun!" by Dr. Jean on CD. This CD offers fun directions of things for the children to do while the song is playing.

"A Sailor Went to Sea, Sea, Sea" from "Just For Fun!" by Dr. Jean on CD. This CD offers fun directions of things for the children to do while the song is playing.

"Baby Fish" from "Dr. Jean Sings Silly Songs" on CD. This song has a fun beat. The children will enjoy singing along to it.

"Five Fish Swimming in the Sea" from "Dr. Jean Sings Silly Songs" on CD. This song has a fun beat for the children to sing along with it.

LANGUAGE AND LITERACY

Fish is Fish by Leo Lionni, Scholastic Inc.

A Day at the Beach by Mircea Vasiliu.

Usborne First Nature: Fishes by Alwyne Wheeler, EDC Publishing.

Sharks! by Catherine Nichols, Hello Reader, Level 1, Scholastic Inc.

The Rainbow Fish by Marcus Pfister, Adapted by Alison James from her translation of The Rainbow Fish published by North-South Books, an imprint of Nord-Sud Verlag AG, Gossau Zurich, Switzerland.

Animals Animals by Eric Carle, Scholastic Inc.

The Biggest Fish by Sheila Keenan, Scholastic Inc.

The Shark Who Was Afraid of Everything! by Brian James, Scholastic Inc., 2002.

Starfish Stars of the Sea by Connie and Peter Roop, Scholastic Inc., 2002.

Wacky Fish by Fay Robinson, Scholastic Inc., 2003.

Fish Eyes by Lois Ehlert, Trumpet Book Edition.

A House for Hermit Crab by Eric Carle, Simon & Schuster Books for Young Readers.

Muppet Treasure Island Treasure Hunt by Lara Bergen, Muppet Press Grosset & Dunlap - New York.

A Day Under Water by Deborah Kovacs, Scholastic Inc.

Whales and Dolphins by Peter and Connie Roop, Scholastic Inc.

The Magic School Bus Gets Eaten by Scholastic Productions Inc. Based on The

Magic School Bus books written by Joanna Cole.

Baby Beluga by Raffi (Raffi Songs to Read) Homeland Publishing a division of Troubadour Records Ltd.

Down by the Bay by Raffi (Raffi Songs to Read), Homeland Publishing a division of Troubadour Records Ltd.

Under the Sea From A to Z by Anne Doubilet, Scholastic Inc.

The Whales' Song by Dyan Sheldon, Dial Books For Young Readers, New York.

Our Day at the Seashore by Amy and Richard Hutchings, Scholastic Inc.

Octopus Under the Sea by Connie and Peter Roop, Scholastic Inc.

The following are teaching tips for reading to children. Make sure that you are well acquainted with the book that you will be reading before reading it to the children. Choose the books that are on the same reading level as the children that are in your class. Use books with colorful pictures and a limited amount of words. Decide what you want the children to learn from the book before you read it to them.

Talk to the children about how you want them to sit or lay before reading. For example, sit up with your legs crossed or lay with your stomach on your mat. You might also say their eyes should be looking at the book and your hands need to be in your lap.

If it is a book where there is a lot of repetition, you may want the children to repeat certain words or make the sounds of animals. Be sure to explain to the children what the signal will be to say the words or sounds. Also tell them what the signal is for them to stop. An example would be, in the book Down by the Bay you would have them sing the repeated chorus with you and hold up your hand with your palm out to show them to stop while you read the verse.

Another thing you might choose to do would be to tell the children to look for simple answers to questions. An example would be for the children to listen and look for how the octopus got away in the book Octopus Under the Sea. Then, after reading the book have them answer the question and any other questions you have asked them. Be sure and have them not answer the question right after asking it, so that they have time to think what their answers are. Say, "Please keep your hands down and think about your answer until I tell you to raise them." Children need to have time to think about their answers.

SMALL GROUP ACTIVITIES/TABLE TIMES

MATH & COGNITIVE

Counting Fish

Before you begin with this activity prepare blue construction papers with simple wave lines and a number written on the end of each paper from 1-10. You may want to laminate them so that they can be cleaned and reused. You also need to buy a box of fish or other sea shaped crackers. Then place a handful by each child in the small group.

Children will count the crackers added to their water (blue paper) one at a time while counting to the numeral on their page. Watch and help children learn when to stop placing the fish so they realize how many represent that number. Start with counting numbers from 1-5. Then, when they are ready to learn higher numbers go to 10 and later to 20 if you are confident that they are ready for a bigger challenge.

Pattern Fish

You may choose to use the same blue papers as in the previous activity. If you do use the same papers, make sure to cover the numbers on them with a sticker, so they won't get confused. For this activity you will need to buy fish crackers or other sea creatures that come in different colors. You could also choose to punch out paper fish or use stickers that have been mounted on small paper squares.

To begin with show the children how to make a two color pattern on the blue paper. Help them add to your pattern the correct colored pieces to continue the pattern you made. Next, have them help you make a new pattern using two different colors. Once they understand what you want them to do, have them make their own patterns.

When children begin to understand the repeating order of patterns, let them try to build patterns using a third color. Work with them to make sure they understand how patterns repeat. Keep going until they can do a four color pattern.

This activity should continue over a period of time and not be done before they understand what a pattern is. This activity will help them learn to see patterns. Point out and explain to them what makes a pattern in art, music, math and writing. This activity can help them in learning how to make their own patterns in math and other areas.

Matching Game

Make cards by using blank 3x5 index cards or use die cuts and your own art or stickers to create the sea animals you want on the cards. Make sure that your pictures are small in size so that you can get up to ten on each card. You can shrink your design by using a color copy machine. Make two sets of cards. Place a number from 1-10 on each card. Turn each card over and glue the same number of sea creatures on the card as the number on the front of the same card. When the cards are finished be sure and laminate them for durability.

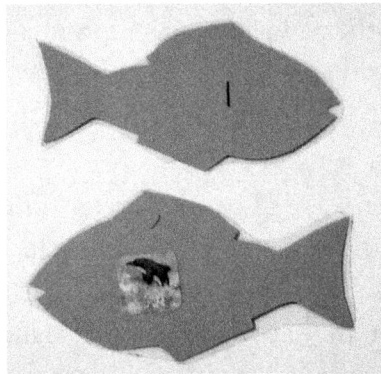

You will want to start by using only the cards that are numbered from 1-5. Place the cards with the numbers face down. Then, have the children take turns placing their finger on each sea item and counting each one on the card. Next, have them turn the card over and say the number with them. Continue on with each of the cards numbered from 1-5. Do this often with the children. Later when a child is able to count accurately, turn the cards over to the numeral side. Then have the children look at each card one at a time and name the numeral. If they say the numeral wrong have them turn the card over and count the figures. Then have them look at the numeral to help them learn how many the numeral represents. Continue using this activity over time.

Once the child is confident with the numerals 1-5, start as before with the image side of the numerals 6-10. They will count the sea items on that side and then turn them over as before to learn how the number matches the amount. Then go on to the numeral side as before. Soon they will be able to recognize and understand that the number symbol represents that amount.

Order Size

Obtain a drawing from a color book, make your own drawing or use clip art on your computer to play this learning game. Choose any sea animal. Copy the animal on a copy machine in four or more different sizes. Cut them out or mount them on paper and laminate them. This will make one set of cards. You can make more sets by using the same animal, but they could learn more if you make two different sets of animals. One animal set could be a long sea animal like a shark and another set could be a tall sea animal such as a whale.

Start out by using only the big and little members of the sets. Ask the child to tell you which animal is the big one and which is the little one. When they can do that have them use the tall/short members and tell you which is short and which is tall. When this has been learned, show three sizes. Use the big, medium and small set placed out of order and have them put them in order and tell you their size names. Practice until they know these well. Next, use the tall, medium and short set out of order. Have the child put them in order and learn their size order names. Now, you can introduce the four figures in each set, one set at a time. You will help the children put them in the correct order from tall/short or long/short. Start at either end of the four objects and say, "What size is this one?" Then point to the next one and say this is the next tallest or shortest one. Continue doing this until you reach the last one. Have them say, "This is the tallest one." If you start the other way then say, "This is the shortest one." Do the same thing with the other set.

Now, you can point out things in your classroom and ask children to show you the longest/ shortest. You might use things like the longest/shortest pencils and tallest/shortest chair. They will enjoy using their new dimensional words.

Match that Shape

Use plain index cards to create game cards. On the front of each card place a shape such as a heart, star, circle, square, rectangle, diamond, oval, octagon or a crescent. Place stickers of sea animals on the back of each shape card. You can draw these shapes, use die cuts, stickers, clip art found on computer programs or trace the shapes from posters found at school supply stores. After you have made two cards for each of the shapes you decided to use, laminate them.

1st game

Mix the cards up and place them on the table face up. Start the game using only three of the pairs of shapes. Have the children take turns finding two cards that match and saying the name of the shape on the card. When the children are familiar with those shapes, gradually add more pairs of the shape cards to the game.

2nd game

Use the same cards as before. Start with three or four different shape pairs. Place the cards on the table with the sea animals facing up and the shapes down. Have the children take turns turning over three cards. They are trying to find a match for one of the shape cards. If they do not make a match, have them turn the cards face down. Tell the children to try and remember where the cards were placed. Then, the next person takes a turn. If they match turn only the card that did not match face down. Continue playing until the last person in your small group has had a turn.

Now, have the children try to make another match. This time if they don't make a match, have them leave their cards with the shape showing. Continue playing in this manner. Make sure they say the name of the shape as they turn a card over. When the children are familiar with those shapes, gradually add more of the shape pairs of cards to the game.

3rd game

First, start with five different shape pairs of cards and shuffle them. Next, tell the children that when it's their turn they will try to make pairs with the cards that they are given. Tell them to hold their cards so that no one else sees them. Then, demonstrate how to play. Example - Ask a child to give you a card in your hand like a circle. Then show your circle. Say its name, "Circle" and place your card with the card you got from the child down in front of you. The child to your right then asks a child for a shape that he/she has in her/his hand. Then, the child says the shape name and places it down in front of her/him. Play continues until all the cards have been placed down.

When the game has been learned and the children are familiar with the shape names, add more of the shape cards.

Find the Treasure

Make a game board on poster board and have it laminated. These are the items to include on your board: a curving line with squares on it, a start area with an arrow, a drawing of a treasure chest for the end, various sea stamps/stickers placed in about eighteen different squares with different instructions written in those squares such as move a certain number of spaces from 1-6, and a ledger at the top showing numerals 1-6 with the number of dots equal to the numeral. See the example of the game board below. You will also need a large die with numbers on it from 1-6. Use small plastic sea creatures or large jewels from a dollar store as markers. Make sure that the markers are different colors or types, so that the children can remember which marker is theirs.

Children play the game by taking turns shaking the die and moving their marker that number of spaces. If they don't know what the number is or how many spaces it represents have them match that numeral to the ledger on the top of the game board and count the dots by it. When they land on a square with instructions on it, they will move that amount before ending their turn. Then, the next person will take their turn. Play continues until all children reach the treasure. The teacher will have a small treasure box with small treats to eat or small toys inside of the box for each child. This will be given out only when all the children in the small group finish, so that the other children that have finished can cheer the others on and help if needed.

✂ FINE MOTOR SKILLS

Ocean Back Drop

Mix food colors or bio paint colors with water and place them into small trigger spray bottles. You can use green, blue, and purple colors. Put large pieces of while butcher paper across the table and let the children spray the paper. It will make interesting colors as they over spray with different colors. You may need to use more than one long sheet in order to cover your bulletin board. The spray bottles help the children gain finger strength. Your other sea projects look great mounted on the paper.

Rainbow Fish

Read the story of the Rainbow Fish before doing this project. Make a fish shape like the one found in the book. Then, cut it out and make tracings of the fish on heavy card stock.

Make several of these for the children to use. Have the children trace around the card stock fish onto a colored piece of construction paper. Then, the next day the children can collage colored tissue squares of tissue paper onto their fish along with small pieces of foil. The foil will be used to make the shiny fish scale the fish had in the story.

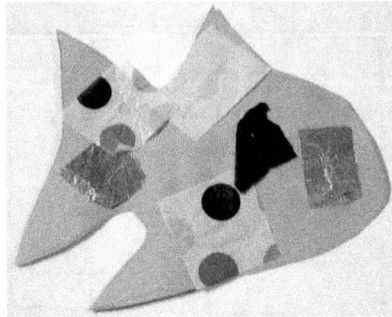

Finger Paint Fish

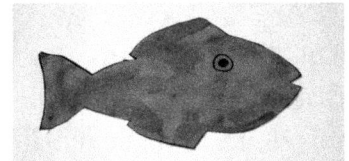

Draw a fish of your choosing and trace it onto the top of large pieces of finger paint paper or plain shelf paper. You can cut out six or more fish at the same time. You will need at least one fish for each child in your class. Write the children's names or have the children write their own name on the back of their fish. You will need to mix one part washable glue to three parts tempera paint. Have the children wear paint shirts or aprons to finger paint their fish. Mix several different colors and place the different colors of paint into foam bowls. When they have finished finger painting on the fish, you can clean up easily by throwing away the paint bowls.

Crayon Relief Pictures

Show the children picture books that have ocean life pictures. Then, pass out watercolor papers to the children. You will need to put crayons out for them to use. Tell the children to draw their own sea creatures. Be sure and tell them to press hard on the paper so that their creatures will show up. Then have them paint a color wash over their drawings. A wash is made by adding an extra amount of water to water colors. Test the wash on a piece of paper to see if the paint is thin and will not block out the crayon pictures. Use blue, green and purple colors. The wax from the crayons will keep the watercolors from penetrating their drawings. The children will be able to create the ocean water for their sea creatures.

Jelly Fish

Make tracers for the children by drawing the body of a jelly fish onto heavy weight paper and then cutting out several patterns. The children will trace around their patterns onto colored construction paper and cut them out. An example is shown below. Next, have them cut out tentacles for their fish. You should have several different colors of crepe paper available for the children to cut to represent the tentacles. Put a masking tape line on the table for the children to measure their crepe paper on and scissors for them to cut it. Next, the children will glue the paper onto the bottom of the jelly fish shape. These jelly fish look cute on the ocean background described before or hanging down from the ceiling. To have them hang from the ceiling, attach fishing line to a tack at one end and to a large paper clip at the other end. The tack goes into the ceiling and the paperclip holds their artwork.

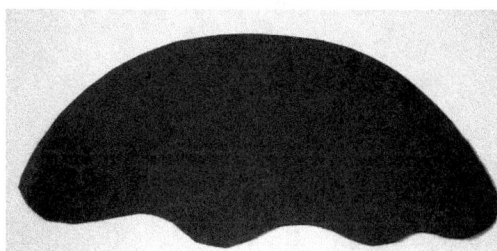

Shell Bubble Prints

Begin by drawing a simple shell shape like the example shown below. Make this into a tracer for the children to use and cut out their own shell or cut them out for them by layering papers to cut several out at one time. If you use white paper for this project the bubble colors will show up better.

To make the bubbles use dish soap such as Dawn. Add water and food coloring or bio water colors to the dish soap. Place this mixture into cereal size bowls and try out the colors to see if they are dark enough by using a drinking straw to blow into the mixture. Once the bubbles cover the top of the bowl, place the shell shape over the bowl to create a print of the bubbles. If it is not as dark as you would like it to be, add more coloring and try again.

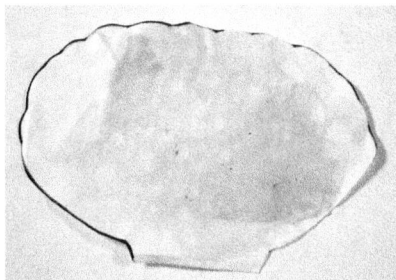

Each of the bowls can be a different color so that the children can move to a different bowl to add different colors to their shell. The colors can over lap on the shell to add interest to their design. Make sure that you remind the children to only use their own straw and to throw it away when they are through blowing bubbles. Also, have them practice using their straw by blowing out of it and feeling the air go out with their hand. Tell them if they suck up they will get the soap into their mouth and it will taste bad.

Star Fish

Give each of the children a piece of construction paper that is light blue, dark blue or green. Have them draw a large star fish for their ocean. They can use white crayons, pencils or chalk so the picture will show up. Then, have them outline their star fish with glue. Next, give them pink, green, purple or gold glitter to sprinkle over it. Be sure and show pictures of real star fish before they begin. This will help them to see how to draw it and all the pretty colors that star fish can be. Sprinkle the glitter inside of a box lid or on a tray so that the unused glitter can easily be poured back into containers when you are finished and be used again.

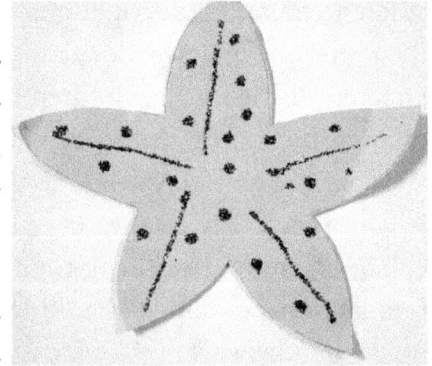

Octopus Headbands

Make simple tracers of an octopus body from cardstock for the children to use as a pattern. Have them trace around the pattern on grey paper and cut them out. Cut out two inch wide bands on a cutting board for each of the children. They will attach their octopus body to the band to create headband octopuses. Have them count and attach eight pieces of grey crepe paper around the headband to represent the tentacles. Use tape to put them on so that they don't have to wait for glue to dry. See example of body.

Lobster

Draw a simple lobster shape and make tracers for your drawing by cutting out your drawing and tracing it on heavy weight cardstock. Cut the patterns out. Have the children trace around the patterns on red and orange colored construction paper. After the children trace them, have them cut out the shapes. Use brads to connect the claws to the top and bottom of the front part of the body. If it is too hard for them to poke the brad through the pieces, then help them press through or use a tiny hole punch to help the brads go through. Then, they can draw on them. Have pictures of real lobsters for them to look at so they can add the details they would like on their lobster.

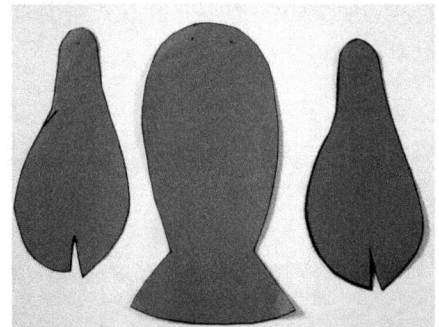

Plaster/Dough Sea Creatures

Use the self-hardening play dough recipe found below or use Plaster of Paris to make shells and other sea animals. An example of the kinds of molds you might use is shown below.

You can find Plaster of Paris at craft stores. You may also be able to buy sea creatures already made there. If you are making your own sea animals use cookie cutters for the shapes. Follow the directions on the bag. Don't use a lot of water. You want the mixture to be thick. Don't leave them in the mold until dry, because it will be too hard to get them back out. Do not use the cookie cutters for any food after using them with plaster of Paris. Candy molds also work well for this project.

If using self-hardening play dough to make the sea animals, you can have the children mold their own shapes such as a fish or sea shell and let them air dry or bake them. The children could also use cookie cutters or candy molds. If using salt dough the molds can be used for food after being washed.

After the sea creatures have dried, children can water color them and you can seal them with a clear sealer. They can take them home to decorate their room.

Self-Hardening Play Dough

4 cups flour
1 ½ cups salt
1 tsp. alum
*Optional 1-2 Tbs. food coloring

Mix the flour, salt and alum together. Then add the the water to it gradually. *If you want mixture colored, add coloring to water before stirring it into the flour. This helps the color to be consistent and smooth.

Stir to form a ball in bowl. Add more water if it won't hold together. Next knead the dough. Place in a sealed container until ready to use. After shapes have been made leave them out to dry.

Easy Fish

Give each child a paper plate and a triangle pattern for the fish tail. Have them place the triangle pattern on the edge of the paper plate and trace around it. Then, have the children cut out this piece and staple it to the opposite side of the plate. This will make the fishes' tail.

Have plastic squeeze bottles such as ketchup containers filled with the special mixture for the children to squeeze out to decorate their fish.

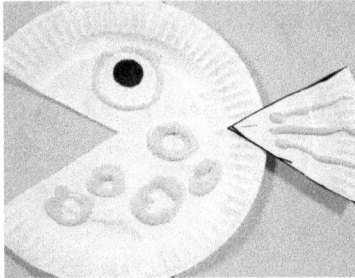

To make the special mixture, add colored water slowly to about 1 cup of salt per bottle. You want the mixture to be thick, but still able to push through the lid on the bottle. Make several colors for the children to use. Let mixture dry flat on the paper plate. It will form a dimensional pattern on the fish.

Whale Art

Cut out a pattern of a large whale such as the one in the example for each child. This can be done by using a pattern from clip art or a coloring book. You may need to enlarge it on a copy machine. Place the desired pattern on top of five sheets of colored construction paper. Trace around the pattern on the top sheet of paper. Place a staple on each side of the stacked paper. Now, cut around the edge and you will have quickly made five whales. Continue as before until you have completed one whale for each child.

Now, set out the different colored whales and let the children chose the color that they would like.

Also set out colored chalk and little bowls for water. The children can dip the chalk into the water and draw on their whale or they can use the chalk dry. You can also encourage children to draw their own whale on plain sheets of paper and color them as they would like.

LANGUAGE AND LITERACY

Shell Game

For this game each child will need their own shell and cup. Shells can usually be purchased from a dollar store if you don't have ones that you want children using. The cups need to be large enough to go over the shells.

This game is used to teach position words like in, on, over, under, beside, in front of and behind.

First, assess which words the children understand by placing the shell in various positions. Then, pick a few of the words that the children need help understanding to work on in this session. You can use the other words at another time.

Say one of the position words, like over the shell, and place the shell over the cup. Then, tell children to place their shell over their cup. Children will continue to place their shell under, behind, etc., as the words are said and demonstrated. Continue playing the game by using some of the words they already understand to give them confidence. Play continues until children are able to follow your directions most of the time. Now tell the children that they will take turns showing and telling the other children where to place their shell. Continue playing until the children have each had several turns. Then bring this game back out another day to continue the learning process.

Fish Card Game

Purchase a set of "Go Fish" cards from a toy department.

Show each of the cards to the children and ask them to say the fish's color or its name if they know it. Tell the children that they are going to play a game where they want to get all the fish that match each other. Tell them that they will all get five cards and that they should put down the fish cards that match each other when it is their turn. Let the children take turns asking another child for a fish card that they have in their hand. They should ask for it by name or by describing how the fish looks. The other children will look in their hand to see if they have a card like the one described. If they do not know if they have it, then the child asking for the card will show the card that he was describing. If the child has that card he will give it to him/her. If the child does not have the card, the child will say, "Go fish." The child that asked and did not receive the card will then pick up the top card off the pile of cards found in the middle of the table and put it into his hand. The child on the right now takes a turn as before. If the child asks has the card, then he can ask for another card as before. This continues until the child draws from the pile of fish cards. Then, the next person to the right takes a turn. Play continues until the pile for fishing is used up. The players may or may not count their pairs. It is best not to have a winner for this game. They are all winners because they described their fish.

Small Group Book Activity

Read the book "Fish Eyes" by Lois Ehlert to a small group of children. Have them count the fish on the pages as you read it. Give them opportunities to express their views about the pictures in the book by asking open ended questions while you read. Next, have the children use paper and markers to create their own fish page. Then, let them take turns talking about their page. Record their comments. Later, combine all the pictures with their comments from the small groups and mount them in a loose leaf book. The next day, read it to all the children.

Picture Pages

Find pictures from magazines of sea animals, the beach, families playing near ocean and other pictures that fit with this theme. Mount the pictures or place them in sheet protector covers, so that they will be protected.

Show each picture to the small group of children and ask them to tell you what they see or what is happening in the picture. Continue by showing each picture and asking children to answer open ended questions about each picture. For example, "What do you think the family is doing in this picture?" "Why are they doing that?" "How do you think you would feel if that was your family?" Be sure not to act judgmental of their answers. Show acceptance of their comments and help them by repeating what you heard and ask things like, "Is that what you meant?" "Can you explain that to me?" "I'm not sure if I understood that." You could also say, "Can you tell me more about that?"

When the children get restless, stop and continue this activity on another day. Let them know that you enjoyed their comments.

Fishing

Prepare by printing the letters of the alphabet on a piece of paper. Make them large so that the children can see them well. You also need to make one fish for every letter in the alphabet. This can be done by using a die cut machine or drawing a simple fish and making more by placing the traced fish on top of five sheets of different colors of construction paper and cutting them out all together. Repeat doing this until you have enough fish.

Now write a different letter of the alphabet on each fish. Use a capital letter on one side and the lower case of that same letter on the other side. Laminate them for durability.

Place a large paper clip on each fish. Buy a dowel stick and a strong magnet at a craft store or hardwood store. Use the stick for a fishing pole by tying and taping a short piece of yarn to the end of the pole. Attach the magnet on the other end of the piece of yarn.

Have the children take turns using the fishing pole to catch a fish. Place the fish with each child's first letter of their name on to a large piece of blue piece of and have them take turns catching a fish. Have them name the letter on the fish that they catch. If they need help tell them that it is the first letter in (name a child's name). Example - K child's name Kim.

Usually, it will only take children a short time to learn the first letter in their name after playing this game and working on it in other ways. Their name is important to them. After they learn the first letter in their name, have them learn the first letter in all their friend's names. Continue on from there to learn other letters and tie them to objects that start with that letter. Example - B for ball. Always say the name of the object with the letter close by it.

Ocean Bingo

Look through magazines, books and/or clip art in software for pictures of shells, fishes, sharks, sea horses, octopuses, seals, whales, star fish, sponges, jelly fish and anything under the ocean that you would like them to learn about. Color copy the pictures in a small, uniform size and place them onto a square poster board. Do not glue them down. You will copy the card with the pictures arranged on the board differently each time. Make as many of each card that you would like and then laminate each card. Keep the individual picture that you use to make the cards to be the call pictures.

Hold up the call picture cards one at and time and show them to the children. Point to each picture and say the name of each of the small pictures. Then, ask the children to tell something they know about any of the pictures. Make sure to take turns giving each child an opportunity to talk. Another day talk about one or more of the pictures and have the children guess which picture you are talking about. After you have briefly talked about all of the pictures the children will be ready to play the game.

Give each child a card and a plastic bag of token covers. The covers can be cereal pieces, beans, fish crackers, gummy fish or anything else you would like them to use to cover the pictures. Tell the children that you will show a picture and they will say the name of the picture with you and match it to the picture on their card. Then, they will cover it with whatever you have prepared for them to use.

Tell them to not look on other children's cards, but look at the picture card you are showing them, because it will be in a different place on their card. When they have a row covered they should say, "Bingo." Then, have the children tell you the names of the pictures that they have in a row. Play continues for a few more rounds and then save it to do again another day. If you would like, you could let them eat the counters that are eatable at the end of the game for that day.

Porthole

Draw a circle and turn it into a simple ship porthole. Then, make copies of it for each child. Place the porthole copies with crayons, markers or colored pencils on the table.

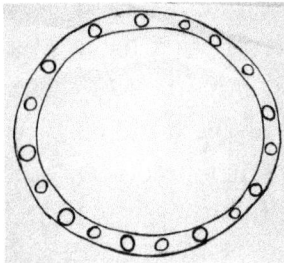

Ask the children to draw inside the porthole what they might see when looking out of it on a ship. When they have finished drawing have them tell you a story about their pictures. Write the story as they tell it to you. If they have few details ask them questions such as, "How big was ..... ?" "How did the .... feel?" "What happened next?" Add the story to the bottom of the picture and read it to the other children. Collect all the picture stories into a loose leaf book and place them in the library section of your room so all the children can enjoy them.

FREE TIME

CREATIVE ARTS

Water Color

Put large pieces of water color paper on the easel. Have the children take crayons and draw pictures of something that they like that lives in the ocean or in tide pools. Tell them to press hard with their crayons to make the pictures dark. Then have them use the green, blue and purple water color paints to paint over their crayon pictures. Make sure you have added plenty of water to the paint. Talk about what happened to the crayon drawings when they painted over them. Put the pictures up on your board for all to enjoy.

Clay

Provide the children with modeling clay, pipe cleaners, popsicle sticks, plastic knifes and pointed sticks. Show the children how to use the tools. For example, show the children how to wrap the clay around a popsicle stick and explain to them that the stick gives the clay strength to hold at different angles. Ask them to think of something from the ocean or nearby it. Have them use the items provided to create whatever they have imagined.

After they have finished their projects have each child dictate to you what they would like others to know about their project. Write their words down on an index card. Put their creation on display in the room with their index card close by.

Table Fun

Put out large pieces of watercolor paper and watercolor paint sets with a cup of water to rinse brushes. Place salt in shakers with tiny holes out for the children to use. Give each child an apron to protect their clothes. The children are going to experiment making an ocean. Have them draw pictures of the ocean with the paints. Before the paint dries have them sprinkle salt on their pictures. The salt does interesting things to the paint that the children will enjoy watching.

Easel Painting

Put large sheets of paper on easels. Give the children poster paint and aprons. Let them paint pictures of ocean and sea life. Have picture books of ocean and sea life nearby to inspire them.

Beach Collage

Place different shapes of blue and tan paper at a table with scissors and glue. Have the children use the items to create their own beach.

Next, let them add a collage of items of their choosing such as sand, sea shells, small colored rocks (found in aquarium supplies), small star fish and anything else you can find that would add interest to their beach.

When they are finished lay them flat to dry. Add the pictures to your bulletin board.

SENSORY

Fill tubs or sensory tables with water. Add bio coloring to the water. Bio coloring is a water base coloring that does not stain like food coloring. You can buy it at school supply stores. Now, add plastic sea animals and fish to the water. You could also add tea strainers to catch fish.

Fill tubs or sensory tables with sand. A great sand to use is called Jurassic Sand. It can be used in water and then dried. It is moldable and has no dust. Add shallow bowls for tide pools. Add plastic star fish to the bowls and anything else you can find that would be in a tide pool. Then add sea shells on the sand areas for them to arrange, count and examine.

DRAMATIC PLAY & SOCIAL DEVELOPMENT

Collect fishing type hats, old fishing rods or dowel sticks with yarn tied to one end and a magnet attached to the other end. Use colored paper fish with paper clips attached to them for the children to be able to catch. Also provide a small basket to place the caught the fish into. It would also be fun to blow up a small rubber boat or raft for the children to fish from. You could use rubber fish instead of the paper ones and have nets to catch them in. The children also could have a small tent on the pretend shore to go home to after fishing. Have old pots and pans and old plates to eat and cook on. If you have large blocks it would be nice to have them close by to create a camp fire. As the children play with the items they will practice and learn to take turns. They can also be taught how to trade items as a good technique for getting along.

SCIENCE

Sink or Float

Prepare a pail of warm water for the children to use in this activity. Also prepare two signs or two pieces of paper. Write the word sink on one sign and float on the other sign with a simple drawing showing something that has sunk and something that is floating. Collect various items from the classroom such as - a pencil, paper clips, an eraser, child's scissors, a crayon, small toys, a wood block, cotton balls, nails, elastics or ping pong balls.

When the children come to the area tell them that they will be scientists and do an experiment to see which items sink and which items float. Pick items and have the children predict (guess) whether the item will sink or float. Explain that scientists use experiments to see if what they predict (guess) is true or not.

Give each child a turn to pick an item and give their guess/prediction. Then have them drop the item in the pail of water to see what will happen. The child will then take the item out and tell what it did. Then the child will place it by the correct sign or on the correct paper. This activity will continue until all the items have been used. Ask the children to look at the area where all the objects that sank are located. Ask the children if they can guess why they all sank. Talk about what was similar about them. Then do the same thing with the items that floated. Help them understand that all the heavy things sank and that the light things floated. If they do not understand this concept keep doing it through the year with different items. Ask more questions and they will get it when they are ready.

GROSS MOTOR SKILLS

Use songs from the CD "All-Time Favorite Dances," by Kimbo Educational. Some of the songs are: "The Chicken," "Mexican Hat Dance," "The Hokey Pokey," "The Conga," and the "Bunny Hop." Also use the song, "The Doggie in the Window" from the CD Young At Heart, by Telarc Digital. Another fun song is found on the CD "Baby Beluga." The title of the song is also named "Baby Beluga." These CD's can sometimes be found at the library. The dances are fun for the children to learn. They want to do them over and over again. During the song "The Doggie in the Window" the children enjoy pretending to be dogs and acting out the song.

Beach Ball

Purchase several beach balls and blow them up. Have the children play catch with each other using them. They can also take the balls outside and hit them up into the air and keep hitting them up so they do not touch the ground. When it touches the ground another person hits the ball up.

Wave Movement

Use relaxing soft music or a real nature music CD of waves. Have the children become waves using long material stripes or crepe paper stripes to move slowly like waves. You can buy soft wave music at most stores that have a section of nature music.

FIELD TRIP IDEAS

The ocean would be a fun place to go on a field trip if you are close to one and have lots of parents that can go with you. If you are far away from the ocean, then a trip to a large aquarium site that features sea water fish and tide pool creatures would be a great choice. Have lots of parents go with you so that you can move with the children's interest. Ask for group rates to make it more affordable.

It's also a good to take sack lunches in coolers. That way after the fun of looking there can be lots of conversations about what everyone saw while they all eat lunch together. It's also a good time to take some group photos of the children with their parents and their friends. Be sure to check out the parks or other places that you could use to eat before you go on the field trip. Plan on bringing table coverings or blankets to eat and sit on. Also, take wipes to clean hands before lunch if there will not be a restroom that they can use. Remind parents to take sunscreen if they will be outside in the sun.

Community Helpers: Postal Workers & Valentine's Day

Talking about Postal Workers and Valentine's Day at the same time works well together. It's fun for children to give and receive mail. This helps them learn how to be a friend. They like to give things to their friends. Encourage children to make and keep friends. This unit will help them learn to be kind to others.

GROUP ACTIVITIES/CIRCLE TIME

🎵 MUSIC AND MOVEMENT

"I Love You" from "I Have A Song For You" by Janeen Brady. There is also a song book by the same title with the simple music in it.

"I Love You" from "Barney's Favorites Vol. 1" CD by Columbia House. This song is different from the song above. It uses sign language with the words to say I love you.

"Singing With Friends" song from tape "Singing With Friends" by Magical David.

"Oh, We All Live Together" from "We All Live Together" Vol. 1 CD by Greg & Steve.

"Friendship March" from "We All Live Together" Vol. 1 CD by Greg & Steve.

"The World is a Rainbow" from "We All Live Together" Vol. 1 CD by Greg & Steve. This is a fun song for the children to act out with their hands and arms. A rainbow is made by moving both arms together in the shape of a rainbow in the sky. The different colors are made by placing one hand up with fingers extended and pointing to each finger as the different colors are sung. When it says, "many kinds of people," point to all the children in your class. When it says, "make the world go around," move your arms in a circle. When it says, "the world is a mixing cup," have one arm in front of you in the shape of a large cup and the other hand/arm doing a stirring movement. When it says, "when we work together," put arms together with elbows bent and fingers extended and sway them back and forth in front of you. When it says, "such a sight to see," make index fingers touch thumb to make circles and place them in front of both of your eyes.

"People In Your Neighborhood" from CD "Young At Heart" by Kunzel.

"Like Me and You" from CD "Quiet Time" by Raffi.

"Mary Wore Her Red Dress" from CD "Quiet Time" by Raffi.

"Looking For Kindness" from CD "Kindness Counts" by Mr. Al and Dr. Becky Bailey.

"Love Is A Circle" From CD "Kindness Counts" by Mr. Al and Dr. Becky Bailey.

"Big Voice" from CD "Kindness Counts" by Mr. Al and Dr. Becky Bailey.

"We All Count" from CD "Kindness Counts" by Mr. Al and Dr. Becky Bailey.

The "Kindness Counts" CD has other great songs on it besides the ones mentioned above. Another great feature is that each song lists activities for you to do with the children while listening to the music.

"Occupations" from CD "Children Love To Sing and Dance with The Learning Station Revised Version!" by Kaladon Publishing. This CD includes the written words to the songs, suggestions and extended activities.

"It's A Small World" from CD "Five Little Monkeys" by Kimbo Educational.

"I Like You, There's No Doubt About It" from CD "Dr. Jean Sings Silly Songs" by Dr. Jean.

This is a short simple song that the children can learn quickly.

"Hello Friend" from CD "Ole! Ole! Ole!" by Dr. Jean in Espanol. This song is sang in English and then repeated in Spanish. It's great for either language and it is a good way to help either language skills along with friendships.

"Twinkle Friends" from CD "Kiss Your Brain!" by Dr. Jean. This CD includes instructions for this fun dance/song. Children love to dance with each other to this song.

"Special Me" from CD "Dr. Jean & Friends" by Jean Feldman.

"What Are Friends For" from CD "Touched by a Song" by Miss Jackie Silberg.

"Share" from CD "Sesame Street – In Harmony."

"Valentine Land" from "Holiday Songs" by MacMillan Program Sing & Learn by Newbridge

Communications, Inc. This is a fun action song where you can have the children pass a paper heart around and when the music stops the child holding the heart goes to Valentine land.

LANGUAGE AND LITERACY

This theme will help children to understand how we get mail and the importance of the mail workers. This theme will also teach that everyone is special no matter what they do as a worker or what color their skin is. Also they will learn that friends can share and take turns.

Heart Activity

Prepare one small heart for each child in the class and write their name on it. Tell the children two weeks before this unit that every day you will be picking a heart from a basket with a different child's name on it. The child who is chosen will be the "special friend" the next day.

The special child will bring an item to show the class. The child will also have a special chair with a sign on it that says, "Special Friend." They will also get to do special things like feed the fish or water the plant. Tell the children that they will all get a turn being the special friend. Give the special child a reminder note to take home the day before their special day.

Tell the children to be thinking about the special child so that they can share something nice about that child the next day. Tell them that they will take turns telling something they like about that child and/or what they like to do with that child at circle time. Example - I like to play with Sammy because he shares the blocks with me.

Write the good qualities on the child's heart and place it on the wall. Help the children identify good qualities the day before so they know what to watch for in their classroom. Here is a list of some of the things that they can become more aware of - sharing, fun to be around, plays with others, nice to others, takes turns, cares how others feel, smiles at others, greets others by saying hello, hugs softly.

The following books are good for circle time. They can help to teach the themes in this section along with using the other materials presented.

I Tell The Truth by David Parker, Scholastic Inc., 2004.

I'm Sorry by Gina and Mercer Mayer, Scholastic Inc., 1995.

Old Henry by Joan W. Blos, William Morrow & Co. Inc., New York 1987.

What Will I Do Without You? by Sally Grindley & Penny Dann, Scholastic Inc., 1999.

Where Is My Friend? by Marcus Pfister, Scholastic Inc., 2001.

I Show Respect! by David Parker, Scholastic Inc., 2004.

Rabbit's New Rug by Judy Delton, Parents Magazine Press. This is a fun book to tell using pictures from the book on small sticks.

Miss Suzy by Miriam Young, Parents Magazine Press.

I'm a Good Friend! by David Parker, Scholastic Inc., 2004.

Don't Need Friends by Carolyn Crimi, Scholastic Inc., 2001.

Friends at School by Rochelle Bunnett, Scholastic Inc., 1996.

It's My Turn, Smudge! by Miriam Moss, Scholastic Inc., 2003.

My Best Friend by P. Mignon Hinds, Golden Books Publishing Company, Inc., 1996.

Friends by Helme Heine, Scholastic Inc., 1996.

What Are Friends For? by Sally Grindsley & Penny Dann, Scholastic Inc., 2000.

Making Friends by Fred Rogers, Scholastic Inc., 1996.

Nathan & Nicholas Alexander by Lulu Delacre, Scholastic Inc.

How I Found A Friend by Irina Hale, Scholastic Inc.,1992.

That's Not Fair by Gina and Mercer Mayer, Scholastic Inc., 1995.

It's Mine by Gina and Mercer Mayer, Scholastic Inc., 1993.

Things to Make and Do for Valentine's Day by Tommie de Paola, Scholastic Inc.

The Valentine Bears by Eve Bunting, Scholastic Inc., 1993.

Valentine Friends by Ann Schweninger, Scholastic Inc., 1991.

Roses Are Pink, Your Feet Really Stink by Diane de Groat, Morrow Junior Books.

Little Mouse's Big Valentine by Thacher Hurd, Troll Associates, 1990.

Clifford's First Valentine's Day by Norman Bridwell, Scholastic Inc., 1997.

Candy Hearts by Rita Walsh, Troll Communications L.L.C., 1997.

Valentine Cats by Jean Marzollo, Scholastic Inc., 1996.

Franklin's New Friend by Paulette Bourgeois, Scholastic Inc., 1997.

Blossom and Boo A Story About Best Friends by Dawn Apperley, Scholastic Inc., 2002.

Community Helpers Mail Carriers by Dee Ready, Bridgestone Books.

At The Post Office by Carol Greene, The Child's World, Inc., 1998.

SMALL GROUP ACTIVITIES/TABLE TIMES

MATH & COGNITIVE

Shapes Heart Game

Make a large heart out of colored construction paper. Draw lines that separate the heart into seven sections. Each section should have a different shape inside. For example, use shapes like a diamond, circle, square, triangle, star, crescent and rectangle. The heart will be the game board. It would be a good idea to laminate the board before you use it.

To play the game, pick a child to close their eyes while another child places a food item like a teddy bear cracker onto a few of the shapes on the heart. Then the child pulls their hand away from the heart and the child with his/her eyes closed opens their eyes. Next, the children say to the child that had their eyes closed, "It's time to open your eyes." The child names a shape that has food on it and if he/she names it correctly then they get to eat the teddy bear on that section. The child continues with each section that has food on it until he/she has tried to name all of them.

Another child is selected to close their eyes while the last child who had their eyes closed is then "it" and places food on different sections of the heart. Play continues as before until all the children have had a turn. You can choose what food treat you would like. Miniature colored marshmallows work well also.

Matching Dots to Numbers

Make two sets of hearts. One set will have dots on each card numbered from 1-10. The second set of cards will have numerals on each card from 1-10.

Children will match the numbers using the dots at first. The numeral cards will be placed in order from 1-10 in front of the child. She/he will pick up a heart with dots on it and count the dots on it. Then they will look at the hearts in front of them and count them to find the one that equals their card they counted with dots on it. They will place the card with dots on it next to that numeral.

Play continues by picking up another dot card and following the order that they did before. The children can do this one at a time from start to finish or they can take turns doing one dot card and match at a time. Complete the game by finding the match to each card.

On another day, have the children put the numeral cards in order and then match the dots cards to the numerals.

Photo Friends

Take photos of children in the class in different size groups from two friends up to ten or more. After they have been developed use them at the math table.

Have children pick a photo and then count the number of friends in the photo. The next child will pick a photo like before and count the friends. Play continues until all the photos have been counted.

Another day have the children at the circle pick a photo card and have them count and pick friends to stand up until they have the same number of friends standing as in the photo. Continue by having another child pick a photo and do the same thing. Keep playing until everyone has had a turn or if it is taking too long, record the names of the people that have had a turn and then tell them the others will have a turn later. Be sure and tell them when they will get their turn and be sure and do it when you tell them.

Racing Bears

Prepare columns on a piece of paper that are made into squares down the page. Have the columns equal the number of friends that you want to be playing as the same time. Four or five at a time is a good number.

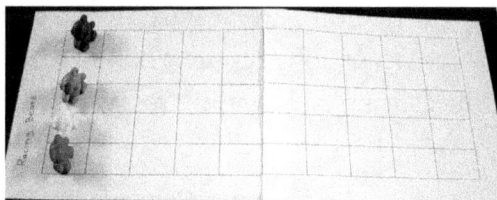

Use bear crackers for markers or any other small thing that you would like. The game starts by having each child place their tokens at the top of their column. Then have the children take turns rolling a die and counting the dots to move that many down their column. The child with their marker in the first column should go first. Then the child with their marker in the next column takes their turn. Once each child has taken a turn, have them start over with the first person again. The children are trying to be the first one to the bottom of their column. They are racing for first place. After the first person makes it to the bottom, stop and have the children count 2nd place, 3rd place and so on. This teaches them about ordinal positions and counting in a new way.

Home Number Matching

Prepare envelopes with the children's name and their number address on them. Make small colored construction houses for each child's address.

In a small group of four children, set out their envelopes and their houses in a mixed up order. Have each child take a turn finding the envelope with their name and address on it. Then have them take turns (with help) saying their numerals in their address. When they each have had a turn telling their numerals, have them match the address on the envelope to the house that has the same address. They will again say their address. Give them help if needed. Next week, play this game again. Review this game once a month so they can learn their address. This game helps them not only to learn their address but, also teaches them that numbers have a purpose.

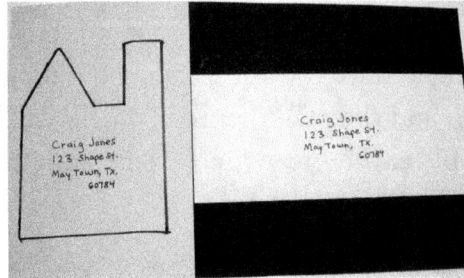

Yogurt Smoothies

Children will learn the importance of knowing numbers in making recipes. They will also learn about sequences. Have the children work in a small group for this activity. They will take turns counting and adding the yogurt, frozen strawberries and measuring and adding the milk. Everyone needs to wash their hands before starting. You will need to have a blender, scraper, measuring cups and ingredients ready.

Strawberry Smoothies

(Makes small tasting cups for 4 children)

Place the ingredients in the blender in the order below.

2 small individual cartons of strawberry yogurt
6 frozen strawberries
¼ to ½ cup cold milk – depending on how runny you want them

Instructions:

Blend until as smooth as you like it.

Use scraper with blender to pour into small cups.

Drink and enjoy.

Have children help put the empty containers in the garbage and wipe off the counter. You will need to wash the blender because of danger with sharp blades.

Smiley Face Counting

Make a set of cards with the numbers one to ten written on them. Make a second set of cards using smiley face stickers. Place one to ten smiley face stickers on each card.

Pass out the smiley cards to the children in your small group. Tell the children when you hold up a number card they should look at their cards and see if they have that same number of smiley faces on their card. If they do they should hold their card. Hold up number cards one at a time until all the cards have been used. Then, collect all the cards and give each child a new card. Play the game again. Be sure and help the ones who need it by assigning partners to play together if needed or use only the one through five numbers.

Heart Categorizing

Make 20 hearts in five different sizes. Divide the children into groups of four. Have each child pick a different size heart and then have them collect all the hearts that are the same size as the one they picked. Next, have the children take turns making a set of the five different size hearts by going in a circle and picking hearts one at a time. Have them arrange the hearts they pick from biggest to smallest. Play continues until all the hearts have been grouped together into a set from biggest to smallest.

FINE MOTOR SKILLS

Valentine Trucks

Each child will be making a Valentine truck to hold the valentines and letters they receive. Provide each child with a piece of extra long (18x12) colored construction paper. Cut out or use punches to provide two, 2 ½ inch wheels for each truck. Have stickers, small punches with colored paper, 1 inch wide strips by 12 inches of paper, markers, scissors, glue and a few tracing pieces for children to take turns using.

Children will choose a large piece of colored paper for their truck and fold it in half. The folded part will become the bottom of the truck. They will place the tracer on one of the top corners of their truck and trace with straight edges on the straight edges of the paper. Then, have them cut the piece off the corner traced. Next, they will write their name on the 1x12 inch strip and glue it onto the truck 1 inch down from the cut off part and even with the sides of the truck. Then, have them glue on their wheels. Now, they can decorate it with punches, stickers and or markers. Teacher will help them close the sides of their truck by using clear tape, glue or staples so it can hold Valentines.

Love Pictures

Place large pieces of white paper, various ½ sheets of colored construction paper, bow tracers, scissors and glue for the children to use, on a table.

Ask the children to draw a picture of someone they love. Then, have them choose a piece of colored paper and trace the bow on it. Next, they will need to cut the bow out and glue it onto their picture. Let them take home their special picture and give it to the person that they drew in their picture.

Heart Picture

Provide a pattern of a large heart on card stock paper for children to trace around. Have them choose a piece of colored construction paper and trace the heart onto it. Then, have them cut out the heart. Using glue, have the children make lines, not big puddles, on their hearts. Give them a large box lid to place their heart into with glue side facing up. Have bottles of glitter in different colors available with small holes for the children to sprinkle onto the glue. Have them cover all the glue with glitter. Then have them carefully lift up their picture and dump off the excessive into the box lid. Place the pictures somewhere flat to dry. Their valentine hearts will look beautiful.

Photo Collage

Give each child a piece of a colored foam sheet that has been cut in half. They will also need a photo of themselves. Place small buttons, sequins, beads, foam shapes, small wood shapes and glue on the table for them to use. Small wooden shapes can often be found in dollar stores with their craft supplies.

Have the children use glue sticks to glue their photo to the foam rectangle. Have them try to place it near the center so that they can place various items around it to create a frame. Let them use a variety of the materials listed to create their frame. When it's dry have them take it to their parents or someone special for Valentine's Day.

Friend Picture

First tape large pieces of paper to the underside of a table. Have each child pick a friend to help them draw a picture. Give them crayons or makers to draw with. Then have them get under the table with their friend. They will lay with their backs on the floor to draw a picture together on the paper that has already been taped to the bottom of the table. When they are finished with their picture they can make one more together. Then they can choose who to give their pictures to or both can keep one.

Love Note

Provide paper, envelopes and markers for the children to write love notes. On a piece of paper write some simple icons that children can copy to write their letter. Some examples of icons would be; pictures of a drawing of an eye for the word "I", a tin can for word "can," a picture of a bee for word be, a picture of a heart for the word love and a picture of a family for word family. Also, write some words on the paper so they can copy them if they want to use them. Examples: Mom, Dad, Sister, Brother, Grandma, Grandpa and baby. After the children have written their letter have them fold it up and put it into an envelope. Be sure and have them put their name on the outside of the envelope, so they won't get their envelopes mixed up. At the end of the day let them take their letters home or you could address them and have the children put on a stamp and place them in a mail drop to be delivered.

Lacing Heart

Go to a hardware store and buy a half sheet of fiber pegboard. You can pay to have it cut into 12 inch squares. Buy some acrylic paint in little bottles at a craft store. Draw a heart shape on each square or draw a few hearts and then put other shapes on other pieces. A few examples of shapes you could draw are a square with eyes and a smile, a circle with a happy face and small circle cheeks and a rectangle with a cowboy hat. After you have drawn the shapes use a small brush with the paint to fill in your design. You can leave it very simple or add lots of details like eyelashes. Then when the paint has dried seal it with a clear spray of acrylic to protect it. Buy long shoe laces from a shoe store. Put the boards and the shoe laces in the classroom. Let the children use the laces to sew through the holes in the pegboards. This activity will build finger strength and hand eye coordination.

Sponge Painting

Buy heart sponges or make your own heart sponges by cutting rectangular sponges with scissors. It is fun to have different sizes of hearts. Mix water based paint from a bottle with dish soap. This will help to keep the children's clothes from staining if they accidentally get some on them. Also, have them wear plastic aprons. Fold a paper towel two times so it is thick. It will act as a stamp pad. Saturate it with the mixed paint. Give each child a piece of construction paper. Have the children place heart sponge onto the paint pad and then onto their paper to make lots of hearts in a design. Use more than one color of paint so that they have a variety of colors to use. Some suggested colors are red, pink, violet, light blue and yellow. This activity can also be done with paper on easels.

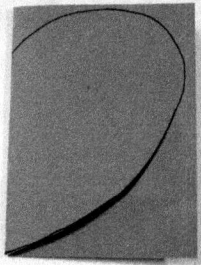

Small Valentines

It is fun for the children to make their own Valentines for their friends in class and then parents will not need to buy them. To make simple ones, show the children how to fold a small square of paper in half and draw a half of a heart on one side of the half with the fold of the paper in the center of the heart. Then, show them how you keep the heart folded while cutting on the line drawn. Open it up to show the heart that was made.

Now, they can make their own with a little help drawing the half heart or you could make a tracer for it. After they have cut out a heart for each child in the class, and this may take a week to do, they are ready to decorate them. Decorating them can be done using lace dollies, stickers, markers, sponge shapes with paint or any other items you can think of. When they decorate them have them sign their name, but not put another child's name on them. It is easier to have them just do the correct number of hearts and have them put one into each child's folder.

Heart Finger Jello

Prepare Finger Jello recipe or make Jello Jigglers the day before you are going to do this activity. You can have the children help you prepare it. They can add ingredients, but not the boiling water. They can also stir the mixture.

Finger Jello – Similar to Jigglers

2 6-oz. pkg. red Jello
5-6 Tb. unflavored gelatin (Knox gelatin)
1 cup sugar

Combine 2 cups water, Jello and sugar. Heat to boiling. Dissolve unflavored gelatin in 2 ½ cups cold water in large mixing bowl. Add hot Jello mixture and 1 cup cold water. Blend well until no crystals remain. Pour into 8x8" pan. Refrigerate overnight.

Next day: Now that the Jello is set up, give the children small heart shaped cookie cutters to cut out a few finger heart shapes to eat. You can also use other small shapes such as dogs, teddy bears, etc.

Friendship Bracelets

Go to a craft store and buy bracelet thread and beads with holes in them that are large enough to easily go through the special thread.

Tell the children that they get to make two bracelets. The first one will be to give to someone in their class and the second one they may keep for themselves. To get started, tape one end of the special thread to the table. Set a bowl with beads in it between every two children. Tell the children to make a pattern with the beads. They should group colors together that look pretty to them. Also tell them not to go to the end of the string or you will not be able to tie the ends together without taking some of the beads off.

When they have finished the first one ask them to give it to a friend in the classroom that has not received one yet. Do this every time to make certain that every child receives one. They can keep the second one. If they don't want to wear it or if they want to give it to someone at home make sure to put it in a folder or bag with their name on it.

LANGUAGE AND LITERACY

Friends Story

Have the children draw a picture about their friends. After drawing their picture let the children take turns showing their picture and telling others the story that goes with their picture. It's nice to record the story on a tape recorder or by writing their words down as they tell the story.

Mail a Letter Game

Put the address of each child on an envelope. Also, prepare a slip of paper with their address on it for use in the game.

Tell the children that each house has a special number called an address. Then, give each child the envelope with their name and address on it. Next, put the slips of paper down that has each of the children in the small groups address on it. Have the children look at the slips of paper and their address envelope and try to match which of the slips has their address on it. Tell the children to look at the letters to see if they are the same as the ones they have on their envelope. Then, have them look at the numbers to see if they match the letters. When they have found their slip of paper with the matching address have them take turns and tell what the numbers are on their address. Now, have the children think about what could be coming in the mail to their house. Then have each child take a turn and tell what they might get in the mail at their house.

Winnie the Pooh

Buy a Winnie the Pooh card game or any other children's card game that has matching cards in it.

Place some of the cards face up on the table and have the children take turns matching up two cards. Have them tell you how they found the two that went together. What did they look for? For example, shape, color or type of animal. In what ways are they the same? Try to have all the children feel good about what they were able to see and say about their cards.

Heart Picture

Make a large heart. Have the children draw pictures of things on the heart that they love and that make them feel happy. Have them take turns telling everyone about what and whom they love and why they love them. Also, have them tell about what and how they make them happy.

Friends

Read the book Making Friends by Fred Rogers. Then talk about ways that they can be a friend to someone. After, let the children role play different ways they can be a friend. You might have one child playing with a toy and the other friend wanting the same toy. Talk about sharing and different ways to do it. Also help them role play what they might do if they didn't want to share right that minute.

Picture Pages

Find pictures from magazines of children and families doing different things. Mount the pictures or place them in clear plastic sheet protectors found at office supply or at scrapbook stores. There is an example shown below.

Show each picture to the children in your group and ask each child what they think might be happening in each picture. Then ask them to look at the faces in the picture and tell about how the people in the pictures may be feeling and how they can tell what they might be feeling. Then ask them to tell how their face looks when they are sad, happy, scared or mad.

Pass Heart Game

Prepare a heart for the game and laminate it. In this game, the children will show that they understand and can use the negative word "not" by playing the game "Pass the Heart."

Have the children sing this song to the tune of "Row, Row, Row Your Boat."

> Pass, pass, pass the heart
>
> As fast, as fast you can.
>
> Pass it to a friend next to you
>
> And see where it will end.

Have the children sit in a circle. Have one child sit in the middle of the circle with her/his eyes closed. The other children will pass the heart around while singing the song above. When the song stops, all the children will put their hands behind their backs. The child that is in the middle will open their eyes and then try to guess who has the heart. Each child who does not have the heart must answer, "I don't have it". The child who has it answers, "I have it". Then the child who had it sits in the middle with his/her eyes closed and play continues again as before. Keep playing the game for a while, but when children are getting wiggly stop the game and tell the children that they will play the game again tomorrow and they can have a turn then being it. Write the names doing that have had a turn being "it".

CREATIVE ARTS

Set the easel up with dark colored paper, colored chalk and small containers of water. Children will dip the chalk into the water and draw with it or they can just draw with it dry. Tell them to draw and/or design whatever they want. The chalk looks and draws differently when it's wet.

Mirror Prints

Place different sized pieces of white and colored paper on the table. You may also add paper shapes such as hearts for children to use. Set out poster paints in a variety of colors. The poster paint works well when placed in plastic squeeze bottles such as catsup and mustard bottles. Then show the children how to fold paper down the middle in either direction they want. Now, tell them to squeeze the paint colors of their choice on one side of the paper and fold the other part over the paint. Next, have them press their hand across the folded paper to smooth the paint under the paper.

Now, have the children carefully open their picture paper and look at their created art work. They always look pretty and each one will be different.

Ice Cube Painting

Prepare ahead of time ice cube trays filled with water mixed with various food coloring in them. It's best to make the colors dark by adding a lot of food coloring to the water. An example of the colors that would be good to use are deep red, dark green, deep purple and deep blue. Place popsicle sticks in each square before putting them in the freezer overnight.

The next day put out white watercolor paper and different trays of the frozen colored cubes. Children will hold the cubes by the sticks and paint on their paper.

Smiley Faces

Set out paper plates, beans and glue. Have the children make a paper plate into a picture of their happy face and then to give it to a friend at school.

SENSORY

Place flour in tubs or sensory table with some of these items: flour sifters, large spoons, small muffin pans, small bowls, small molding pans and small bread pans. Provide aprons for the children to wear while discovering the items in the tubs or table.

Teacher can also use sand in the tubs or table with "Lego's" to build houses "Lego" people to pretend with. The children can build their town on the sand and have the people interact.

Another idea would be to use rice in the tubs or a table with farm animals and popsicle sticks to make fences. Children can also create houses with the sticks at the table by gluing them together to use with the animals when the glue has dried.

You can also place the play dishes in the tubs or table with soap and sudsy water for them to clean.

DRAMATIC PLAY & SOCIAL DEVELOPMENT

In one corner of the room set up a post office. Use a cardboard box to make a large mail box for children to place their mail. They can write/draw pictures and place them in the mailbox. Children can prepare the box by painting it red and blue using poster paint.

Have the children help you collect shoe boxes to be used for individual mail boxes. The pretend mail workers will take the mail from the large mail box and deliver it to the individual boxes. The children can color and glue items on their box to decorate them.

At a small table place envelopes and paper with pens and colored pencils for the children to use for making their letters. Also cut or punch small squares from colored construction paper for them to use for stamps. Have glue sticks available for the stamps. Also provide small boxes to place items in to be mailed.

At a different small table near the large mailbox provide a place for the mail workers to set up shop. Place a scale to weigh boxes, pretend stamps with glue sticks and a cash register with play money. The uniforms can be simple men's blue short sleeve shirts with ball caps for hats. You can usually buy these at thrift stores. Then you can make mail bags from material. See the example below. You could also buy recycle bags used for shopping and use them for the mail bags.

Children will enjoy using this center all year or as long as you desire to have it up.

SCIENCE

Show the children a stethoscope. Tell them what it does and who uses it. Then show them how to use it to listen to someone's heart. Also show them how to care for it. Let children take turns during the day listening to a friend's heart beat.

Another idea would be to place different types of rocks out for them to investigate using a small dish of water with a dropper, a small amount of salt to place on different rocks and a magnifying glass.

Another fun activity to use would be a tape recorder with a blank tape. Show the children how to care for and use the recorder. Children can come to the table with a friend and record songs together or tell stories together and then play them back to listen to them.

Bring in a model of a heart and show the different parts. Tell children in brief terms how the heart works. Then let them examine the heart themselves during the day.

Bring in an inexpensive camera and show how it works. They can each have a turn taking pictures of their friends. When the roll of film has been used up, develop the film and place the pictures out for the children to say the names of the children in the pictures.

Another idea to do for science would be to use magnets. Teach the concept of magnetic forces and relate how friends can stick together like the magnets. Also teach that if we are unkind to our friends they are drawn away from us like the magnets when turned the other way. Let the children experiment with the magnetic forces.

GROSS MOTOR SKILLS

Have the children sing words and do actions to the song, "If Your Happy and You Know It." This song is found in many variations on CDs, tapes and sheet music. You can start with the basics – "If you're happy and you know it clap your hands" and move on to your own verses such as – If you're happy and you know it hug your neighbor, jump up and down, swing your foot, pull a face, shout hooray, touch your toes and many other actions. The children really enjoy doing the actions and the song is simple for them to sing.

Another fun activity for them is to use a parachute or a large sheet. Have the children hold on to the sides tightly and tell them to only move up and down when you say. Practice following directions before doing this to music. They can also hold it tight and while pulling it taunt walk around in a circle. When they get good following directions you can have them shake it up and down as fast as they can and you can also have them go up and down together while having soft foam balls on top of it. They love these activities.

FIELD TRIP IDEAS

Arrange ahead of time to have the children go to a post office. Have the children write letters or draw pictures for their parents before doing this activity. Make sure to address the letters before the field trip.

Ask the staff to show the children how the mail is collected from the mail box and how it is taken to the sorter. Also have them show the children how the stamps are canceled. Have them show the boxes that are for rent at the office and how the mail is put into their boxes. Have them show the children the backs of the boxes where they place the mail and the keys that the customers use to open their boxes. Tell them that most people have their mail delivered to their home mail box. Be sure and also show them boxes that will be delivered and ask them if their family has ever gotten a box in the mail.

Have the children watch as you purchase stamps for their envelopes. Give each child a stamp and show them where to put the stamp on their envelope. Next have them put their letter through the slot to mail it.

Next give the post office helpers a big poster saying thank you from all the children. You could have them all sign it or trace their hand print on it before the trip.

When they return back to the school have the children draw pictures of what they saw at the post office or have them draw a box showing what they would like to be delivered to them.

More Community Helpers: Carpenter, Librarian & Barber

GROUP ACTIVITIES/CIRCLE TIME

MUSIC AND MOVEMENT

"The Corner Grocery Store" from tape/CD, "The Corner Grocery Store" by Raffi. The children enjoy going to their corner grocery store. This is a fun song that tells about some of the foods found there. Make cards to help them learn the words.

"Mr. Knickerbocker" from "Barney's Favorites" Vol. 1. The words to this song are included with the tape along with the actions to do with the song.

"People in Your Neighborhood" from "Sesame Street" by Columbia in cooperation with Children's Television Workshop.

"To the Barbershop" from "Macmillian Sing & Learn Program" by Newbridge Communications, Inc. Children will sing the simple verse and use different movements each time they sing the song. Example - Hippity hop to the barbershop, Jumpity jump jump to the barbershop and so on. The children will do these activities while singing this song.

"Mr. Weatherman" from "Macmillian Sing & Learn Program" by Newbridge Communications, Inc. Children will sing the song and pretend to dress different ways for the weather that the weatherman tells them the weather will be like that day.

"Barbershop Song" from "Macmillian Sing & Learn Program" by Newbridge Communications, Inc. Children will act out the words in this song.

"The Doctor" from "Macmillian Sing & Learn Program" by Newbridge Communications, Inc. In this song the children will play a game. The directions for this song are included with this song tape.

"Fire Fighters!" from "Macmillian Sing & Learn Program" by Newbridge Communications, Inc. Children will sing the song and act out driving to different places where a fire has been located so they can put out the flames.

"The Traffic Cop" from "Macmillian Sing & Learn Program" by Newbridge Communications, Inc. Children will sing the song and act out directing the traffic.

"The Bus Ride" from "Macmillian Sing & Learn Program" by Newbridge Communications, Inc. Children will sing the song and do the actions in the song.

"At the Library" from "Macmillian Sing & Learn Program" by Newbridge Communications, Inc. Children will sing and learn what you do at the library.

"911" from "Macmillian Sing & Learn Program" by Newbridge Communications, Inc. Children will sing and pretend to be calling the number.

"Oh Hey Oh Hi Hello" from "Jim Gill Makes It Noisy in Boise, Idaho." This is a fun greeting song that uses their voice in making it happy, sad and many other ways.

"Five Little Monkeys" from "Five Little Monkeys Songs for Singing and Playing." Children will enjoy singing and doing the actions to this fun song.

"It's A Small World" from "Five Little Monkeys Songs for Singing and Playing." Use this song as a reminder that we are all the same in that we all enjoy laughter, we all cry and we all have hopes and fears.

"I'm a V.I.P." from "I Have A Song For You" CD by Brite Music Enterprises, Inc.

Use this little song to help children remember the emergency number. Sing it to the tune of "I'm a Little Teapot"

> I am a Police person
>
> with a badge.
>
> I help people near and far.
>
> If you have a problem
>
> call 911
>
> and I will be there fast.

LANGUAGE AND LITERACY

My Tall Book of Happy Town by Sandy Damashek, Published by Playmore Inc., Publishers and Waldman Publishing Corp.

Corduroy's Busy Street/Corduroy Goes To The Doctor by Don Freeman, Vicking Penguin Inc.

How Emily Blair Got Her Fabulous Hair by Susan Garrison, Bridge Water Paperback, 1995.

Check It Out! The Book About Libraries by Gail Gibbons, Harcourt Brace Jovanovich, Publishers.

Busy People All Around Town by R.W. Alley, Merrigold Press.

The Paperboy by Dav Pilkey, Scholastic Inc., 1996.

I Stink! by Kate & Jim McMullan, Scholastic Inc., 2002. This is a story of a garbage truck and teaches appreciation for the workers of the city's department of sanitation.

<u>I Took My Frog to the Library</u> by Blanche Sims, Puffin Books, Published by Penguin Group, 1990.

<u>At the Library</u> by Christine Loomis, Scholastic Inc., 1993. This book shows a lot of fun things that you can do at the library.

<u>All About Things People Do</u> by Lesley Smith, Scholastic Inc., 1998.

<u>Walter the Baker</u> by Eric Carle, Scholastic Inc., 1996.

<u>My Apron</u> by Eric Carle, Scholastic Inc. This is the true story of Eric Carle learning to help his uncle lay bricks.

<u>Mike Mulligan and His Steam Shovel</u> by Virginia Lee Burton, Houghton Mifflin,, 1977.

<u>Building a House</u> by Byron Barton, William Morrow, 1997.

<u>Construction Zone</u> by Linda Hayward, Dorling Kindersley, 2001.

<u>I Want to Be a Chef</u> by Stephanie Maze, Harcourt & Brace.

<u>When I Grow Up</u> by Colin McNaughton, Candlewick Press.

<u>A Carpenter</u> by Douglas Florian, New York: Greenwillow, 1991.

<u>Bruno the Carpenter</u> by Lars Klinting, New York: Holt, 1995.

<u>A Day in the Life of a Carpenter</u> by Liza N. Burby, New York: Rosen 1999.

<u>When I Grow Up</u> by Rosemary Wells, New York: Hyperion, 2003.

<u>I Want to Be A Fashion Designer</u> by Mary R. Dunn, Powerkids, 2009.

<u>Froggy Bakes A Cake</u> by Jonathan London, Scholastic Inc., 2000.

<u>The Home Depot Big Book of Tools</u> by Kimberly Weinberger, Scholastic Inc.

SMALL GROUP ACTIVITIES/TABLE TIMES

MATH & COGNITIVE

Patterning

The teacher will draw a saw, hammer and a wrench or use clip art for pictures of these tools. Then duplicate the pictures and place them on poster board paper. You will need three of each picture per set. These cards can be cut into 3x3 size and laminated. You will need one set for each child in your small group. Show the children how to make a simple pattern by repeating how they are laid out. Example: one saw, one hammer and then one wrench repeated. Then tell the children to make a pattern with their squares and keep repeating it until all their pattern pieces have been used. Help them if they cannot figure it out. If they can do it, have them make another pattern.

Emergency Numbers

Make cards with individual 911 numbers on them. Have the children say the numbers with you. Then mix up the numbers and have the children take turns putting them in the correct order while saying the numeral names.

Now, use a real phone that is not plugged in and have the children practice dialing the phone. Be sure and stress that this number is not to be dialed when someone big can do it for them. Playing on pretend phones is okay, but real phones can cause someone to not get the help that they need in an emergency.

Racing Game

Place a lump of play dough on the table with a stick of uncooked spaghetti standing up in it in front of each child in your small group. Also place different community helper hats on table for children to choose. Examples of hats are: construction, baker, fireman, police and hard hat.

Have the children pick a hat to wear for this race. Give each child a handful of fruit loops or Cheerios, at least ten. Tell them that when you say go they must place the number of cereal pieces on the spaghetti that you say up to ten. Then after everyone has had time to put them on everyone will stop and take turns counting how many that they have. The children with the correct number on their spaghetti will be the winning community helper/helpers. Do this a few times with the same group saying different numbers for them to place on and then let others come over to play the game.

Cash Register Game

Provide a toy cash-register and pretend pennies for this game. These can be made by punching or cutting small circles out of poster board and writing the number one on each of them. Make enough coin so that each child in the small group can use a bag of 10 coins.

Prepare small items such as toy cars, stuffed animals, playing cards, notebooks, decorated pencils and anything else you can think of that is cute and small. Then tape a sign on each item with a number between one and ten for the number of cents.

Tell each child that they will take turns being the cashier and the customer. They will pay for each item with the correct number of pennies marked on the item. The cashier will count the money that they give him/her to see if it is the correct amount and place the correct amount in the cash-register. Then they will place the item in a bag. Tell the children that they will not be able to keep the items because they belong to the school. When each child has had a turn pretending to buy an item, one of them will be the new cashier. They will put their items back and be given a bag with coin in it again. Now they will start the game over again. Play continues until everyone in the group has had a turn being the cashier.

Save the House

Make a game board that starts with a fire engine and ends at burning house. Use rectangle or square shapes between the house and the fire engine. Write numerals on the pieces and put a corresponding number in each one. Arrange and glue them on to a piece of poster board. Then have it laminated. Use a large die and cover its dots with numbers. Prepare game tokens for the children to move. They can be any small item with a flat bottom such as Fisher Price person, a small toy fire engine or a square shaped craft glass piece used in a vase.

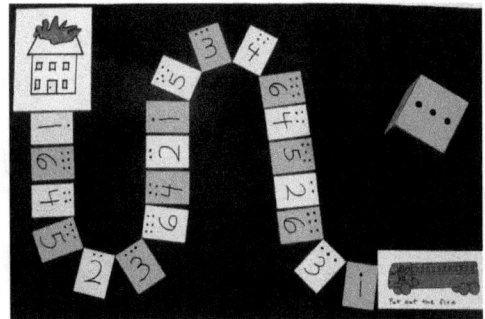

Have the children take turns rolling a die. Play will begin by saying the number or counting the dots and then saying the number. Then they can move their token that many spaces. The next player will then roll the die and continue as before. The game will keep going in the same manner until one of the children get to the burning house and saves it.

FINE MOTOR SKILLS

Wood Building

Obtain a scrap of wood from a building supply store (such as The Home Depot), wood craft outlet or a construction site. Be sure and ask first and explain that it is for preschool children. You will also need to purchase wood glue and save cardboard boxes. Cut off the box sides to use for the bases on the children's wood projects.

Have children sit at the table and explain to them that they can use the boards and glue to create something that they would like. Tell them to put their project on the cardboard so that they can be moved to dry when they are finished designing their project. Also tell them that when it is dry they can paint it how they would like.

Nail Painting

Provide papers, pencils and pretend nail polish. You can use real nail polish, but you will need to get parent's permission for the children to have polish on their nails. I use the pretend kind because they don't try to polish their own nails and you have lots of different colors with little cost.

To make pretend nail polish, save your old small bottles of glue. Mix a little poster paint into the bottles or use bio coloring and shake to stir the mixture up. Use old water color brushes for the painting.

Have the children trace around their hands with a pencil on their paper. Then let them paint the ends of the traced fingers with the pretend polish. They can paint each finger different or all of them the same. This project goes along with talking about what they do in salons.

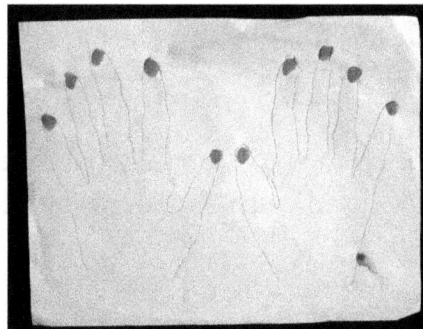

Hair Design

Supply a paper plate and a hole punch for each child. Have the children use the hole punch to punch holes in the top edge of their paper plate. They can be close together or far apart, but explain that this is where their hair will be.

Next let the children choose the pieces of cut yarn that they would like for their hair. You can have cut out pieces of hair about sixteen inches long each or the children may cut their own yarn hair in a length of their choosing.

Show the children how to fold the yarn over and poke it in through one hole. The folded piece will go through the hole first about 1 inch. Then the folded piece will thread through the loop made with the yarn end. Pull the long thread flat and they will have the first of their hair fastened to their head. Continue in this manner until all the holes have yarn through them. Now decide where to draw the eyes, eye brows, eyelashes, nose and mouth. Use crayons or markers for this job. They might also like to draw hair for bangs or sideburns.

Face Shaving

Boys and girls all like to do this activity. Buy sensitive type shaving cream. Also have mirrors, aprons and craft sticks available for the children. Caution the children to keep the shaving cream away from their eyes and mouth. Have the children wear aprons for this activity.

Give each child a small mound of the shaving cream. Have the children use the mirrors and their fingers to carefully place the cream on their cheeks while keeping it away from their eyes. Then have them use the flat side of the craft stick to shave the cream down off their faces. After each scrape down they will wipe the stick off with their finger. When they are through shaving they will go to the sink and use a paper towel with warm water to wipe off their face and dry them.

If you think they might not be able to do it carefully, have them shave baby doll faces or use a foam plate turned upside down with a face draw on it to shave.

Book Making

Set out colored construction paper, white copy paper, stapler, markers, and crayons. Show the children how to fold the construction paper in half to make a book cover. Then have them fold one or two pieces of copy paper in half and place them inside the colored construction paper and staple them down the fold to make a book. Now have the children think about what they would like their book to be about. Then have them draw pictures on the blank white pages to tell a story of their choosing. If they would like help with writing their story, write their words for each of their picture pages. Have the children tell their story to others in the class and place it your library at school. Later have them take it home to read to their parents.

Wood Design

Give the children colored construction paper, glue, toothpicks, wood craft sticks in thin and wide sizes and colored wood shapes. These items can be found in dollar stores and craft shops. Tell the children to place them on their paper they way they want them to look and then to glue them down when they like the way that they have been arranged.

Muffin

Make a large muffin pattern and place it over five pieces of paper and cut them out all at one time. Continue to use the same procedure to make enough muffins for the class. Give the children the shape and water colors to paint their own design on the muffins.

Barber Coat

Draw a simple outline of a barber coat onto a large piece of butcher paper. If the butcher paper is light weight you can place it over the drawing and trace it on to the next page. If you can't see through it, just keep the drawn coat close to the blank paper and make it the same proportions as the first drawing.

Make one for each child. Also mix different colors of poster paint and place on a foam paper plate. Buy or bring out all the shape cookie cutters you can find. Have paint aprons on the backs of the chairs as a reminder to wear them when painting. Children will dip shapes of their choosing into the paint and then stamp them on to the barber coat. Children may design the shapes in any order on their sheet and use any colors of paint. This activity helps them develop eye hand coordination.

LANGUAGE AND LITERACY

First Aid Bags

First gather these first aid materials - Band-Aids in different sizes, foil wipe packages, and small plastic zip lock bags. Ask the children what each of the items are and how they are used. Then use questions to talk about when it's used and how a bandage should be used. Talk about germs and dirt entering into a break in the skin. Talk about the job that the wipes play. Ask when you would use them and why you would use them. Then have the children practice using a wipe and a bandage on a doll. Next talk about the different sizes of the bandages and ask how they know which size to use when one is needed. Now pass out a zip lock bag, one bandage in each of the different sizes and four foil wipe packages for each child to have. Have the children place the items in their bag. The children will place these items in their backpack to use when needed. Be sure and let their parents know about this project.

Same and Different Game

Prepare cards with pictures or drawings of items or use real items that they can handle. The types of the items collected will be from the community helper theme that you are discussing. For example, if you were learning about a carpenter you could use two different types of screwdrivers, a Phillips and two standard screwdrivers. Show the cards or the real tools and ask the children what each item does. If they do not know, talk about and demonstrate how each item is used. Then, show the standard screwdrivers and ask the children if they are the same or if they are different from each other. Next, put the standard one by the Phillips one and ask if they are the same or different. If they still don't get it have them look to see what parts are the same between the three items and what parts are different. Now, use this same technique using other tools such a two bristle paint brushes and one sponge paint brush.

Emotions

Draw a picture of a boy and another one of a girl. Place each one in the center of a poster board.

Have the children come to the small group area and look at the drawings. Take turns asking each child to make a comment about either the boy or the girl. Write the comments on slips of paper and tape them by the picture of what the child commented about. For example, she has dark hair or he has blue eyes.

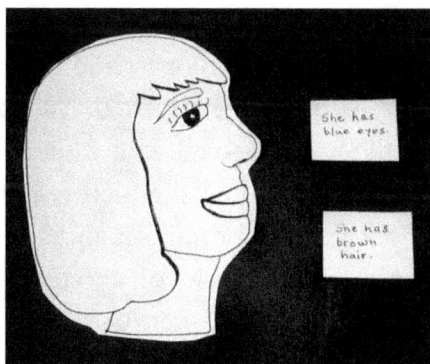

Then, ask the children to think about the different ways the boy or girl can feel. Take turns again writing the different feelings that the children think up. Help them realize that we all have many different emotions.

Next, ask the children to take turns telling what can make the boy and/or the girls feel the different ways that are listed. After going through their ideas of why the boy and girl felt that way ask them if it is okay to feel those different emotions. Let them know it's okay to feel all the different ways, but it's not okay to hurt others.

Discuss different things that they can do without hitting or using bad hurtful words. Such as saying to the child that took your toy, "I don't like it when you take my toy. It makes me feel sad." They might say, "Give me back the toy and I will let you have a turn when I through with it" or they could say, "We can play with it together." Tell them that this doesn't always work with the other child, but it can help them express their feelings and let the other child learn how the other child feels. They can also learn sometimes it's best to walk away and find something different to do if they have expressed themselves and it doesn't work.

Story Order

For this activity, you will need to buy cards from a school supply store or make your own cards. This is an activity a child might do in three parts. For example, the first card would show a picture of a child sitting by wood beads. The next card would show a picture of the child putting a bead on a long string. The last card would show a child with all the beads on a necklace. If you don't feel that you can draw the pictures look for pictures in coloring books of things a child has done. Start backwards with what was done (card 3). Then use the simple lines in the coloring book to help you trace the step that happened just before (card 2). Then draw what happened before that (card 1). You will have the three steps. You can also get someone to draw some figures for you. Often people that aren't professional will feel flattered and be happy to help you out. You can also make cards by taking photos of children doing various things like building with blocks. Once you have obtained several different sets of cards laminate them so they will be sturdy.

Now you are ready to work with the children one child at a time. Mix up a set of cards and have them put them in order of what happened. When they are through placing them in order ask them to use their words to tell you what is happening in each picture. If they get it wrong ask more questions about the pictures to try and help them see the order. If they still don't see it move on to another set and see how they do with different pictures. Now tell them thanks for playing with you and tell them they can go do another activity. Call another child over to play with you. Continue until each child has had a turn. See the example of Scholastic cards that you can buy.

Story Recall

Prepare several pages with different pictures on each of them. Try to collect pictures from magazines that will be interesting to the children. Then write a short paragraph about the picture. Mount the picture on a sheet of card stock and the paragraph under it. You can laminate the pictures of slip them into plastic sheet protectors.

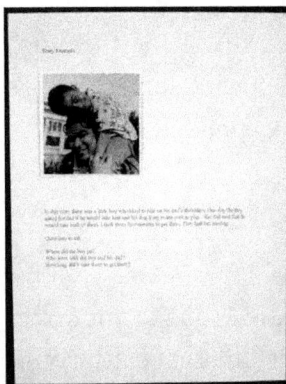

Now have children come to you one at a time. Tell the child that you are going to show them a picture and tell them and story. Also tell them that you will be asking them a few questions after the story about what happened. Ask them to listen carefully.

The teacher should choose the questions for the children to answer before starting and keep the same questions for each child. Keep a record of the child and how many of the questions they got correct for each picture, but only do one picture story at a time. At a later time do the activity again and see if the child has made progress. Record the progress of the child so you know what to do to help the child.

FREE TIME

CREATIVE ARTS

Glitter Art

Set out various pieces of cardboard that you have cut from cardboard boxes. Also set out containers of different colors of mixed poster paint and shaker bottles of glitter. Have child size aprons available for their use as well as cardboard box lids for them to place their pictures in. Let each child paint a picture on a piece of cardboard. While the paint is wet have them set their picture in a cardboard box lid and shake glitter on it. When the pictures are finished put them on the counter to dry.

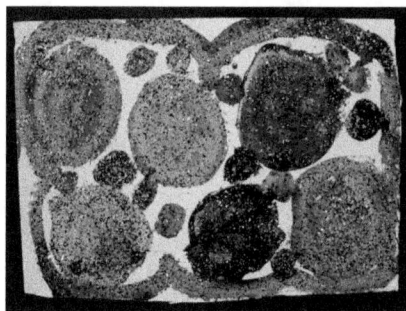

Easel Art

Set up the easel with paper and place water color sets with water in the tray. Encourage the children to paint whatever they would like. Explain to the children that they need to rinse out their brush in the water before using a different color so that they can have many colors to work with. Show the children a box of paints that hasn't been used properly so they can see that the colors are only brownish black now. Have them also change the water cup with clean water when it is dirty and when they are finished painting for the next child to use.

It would be appropriated to have various picture books close by so children can find something that they would like to paint. The books can show designs or pictures of different things. The author and artist Eric Carle are good books to set out because the pictures have all been painted by him and they can see the brush work.

Bakery

Make white play dough for the children to use to create bread, cookies, cupcakes, rolls and more using rolling pins, plastic knives, miniature or small muffin tins and bread pans. If possible, small pizza pans and plastic roll cutters would be fun for them to use along with different texture items that can make impressions in the dough.

Play Dough

2 cups flour	2 Tbs. cream of tartar
1 cup salt	2 Tbs. cooking oil
2 cups water	*food coloring optional

Combine all ingredients in a medium sauce pan. Mix well. Cook over low heat stirring constantly until mixture gathers and forms a dough. Dump onto counter until cool enough to handle and then knead to form a ball. Store in a container or plastic bag.

*Food coloring may be added to the water before. Mixing with the flour.

SENSORY

Flour Fun

Fill the sensory table and\or tubs with flour. Have flour sifters, spoons, small bowls, small loaf pans and muffin tins available for this fun activity to encourage your little pretend bakers. You can also use candy molds in the flour. Be sure and have aprons for them to keep their clothing clean and give clear directions of what they can do before playing in the flour.

Wood Shaving

Another fun thing to put into the sensory table is wood shavings. If you can't find a place to give it to you for free then you can go to a pet store and buy it there. Wood shavings are used for some types of pets to put in their cages. While you are there you can buy several toy pets and accessories to put in the bedding at your school. The children will enjoy having a pretend pet to care for and play.

DRAMATIC PLAY & SOCIAL DEVELOPMENT

Library

Use your book area and turn it in to a library. Place a table next to the books with a clip board for papers and pencils. Have the children write their name on the paper when they check a book out. Have pillows on the floor for them to sit and read their book on. When they are finished with their book have them take their book back and draw a line through their name.

Salon

Step up an area where they can pretend it's their salon. Have a front desk with a cash register, play money, phone, notebook to make appointments on, pencils, and a clock to tell when it's their turn for their appointment. Have chairs set up in a line with magazines for the customers to look at while waiting. Save and clean shampoo bottles, rinse bottles, pump hair spray bottles, after shave bottles, empty make-up containers and make-up brushes. Other items to include could be hair dryers and curling irons with their cords cut off. Wigs and other things for their hair like barrettes could also be included. It would be good to include caps for them to wear under the wigs while they get their hair done. You can use combs and brushes for wigs too. Don't use combs and brushes for children unless each child has their own with their name on it so children are protected.

Place all the bottles and other things you have accumulated in their salon. Also have a special chair for them to sit on and a mirror to look in. You can make it look special by placing a paper sign on it or slipping a child size pillow case over the back of the chair with a star on it.

Construction Area

This can be an area with hard hats, a work bench with tools, goggles and pieces of wood. It can also be enhanced with glue and colored markers. This area can also include wood blocks and or cardboard blocks. It would also be fun to add simple blue prints if you have time to make some. Other items to add would be cardboard boxes with masking tape. There could also be a place outside for them to take their creation to be painted. Have poster paint with regular small paint brushes to paint the boxes.

SCIENCE

Yeast

Place dry yeast in a bowl with warm water and see what happens. Now get a bowl with cold water. Have the children guess what might happen to this bowl. Place dry yeast in the bowl with cold water. Talk about what happened. Then use a bowl with warm water, yeast and add 1 teaspoon sugar to the yeast and have the children predict what will happen. Next children will use warm water, yeast and 1 teaspoon salt. Have them predict what will happen. Children will be lead by the teacher to see similar things that happened and decide which two methods helped the yeast to grow. Then help them see which action helped the yeast to grow the fastest. Another time they could experiment to see what other things could make the yeast grow or not grow.

Seed Experiment

Buy grass seed, sponges, small spray bottles and a clear plastic shoe box for this experiment. Prepare the box by soaking the sponges in water and placing them into the clear box. Then cut them to fit the entire bottom of the box.

Have the children take turns sprinkling the grass seed on top of the sponge. Have them spray them with the small water bottles daily. The box should be placed on a table or shelf by the window. Place a paper on a clipboard by the seed box. Have the children predict if the seeds will come up by writing their name under a column of yes or under no. Next to their name on the yes side have those children make a guess of how many days it will take for the seeds to come up. Help them write the number and make a small line next to that number that will be the equal the same amount of days that they guessed. Every day the children will check the box to see if they have come up or not. Pick a child to draw a line for everyday that they have not come up. This will continue until the seeds have come up. On the day that the seeds come up help the children count their marks to see how many days it took for them to come up. Then read each person's guess for when they would come up and help them determine which child came closest to the date that they came up.

GROSS MOTOR SKILLS

Red Light Green Light

Make two circles on red and green construction paper and attach them to a craft stick. Explain the game to the children before going outside to play it.

Have the children stand in a horizontal area that is the starting place. You should stand at the opposite end about 30 feet away or where it will work under your circumstances. Take several turns to be "it" so that the children can learn to play. Start by alternating between showing the red and green lights. The children should run when the green light is shown and stop when the red light is shown. When a green light is shown point to the children that keep moving and send them back to the start. After a few rounds let the first person to touch you take a turn to be "it." The object of the game is to be the first one to touch the person that is "it." The first person will then get a chance to be "it."

Another time to add variety you could have the children do other things instead of run. You could have them hop one foot, jump with feet together, skip, take giant steps, take baby steps, and walk on tip toes.

Balloon Bating

Make a bag with material that is just about twelve inches wide and about fifteen inches long. Fold the material right sides together with the sides together. Now sew each side together. This bag will be used to hold balloon. Cut a strip of material about two inches wide and twelve inches long. Fold it with wrong sides together so that long edges are even. Now do a zig zag stitch down the edge. This will be used to tie the top edges together or you can use a piece of ribbon for the tie. Blow up a balloon and place it inside the bag. Tie the bag closed with the long fabric piece or a ribbon. This is for safety to protect the children from a popped balloon that could cause choking. Now make bats. Use duct tape to attach wood paint stirrers to paper plates. You can use a wood stapler to attach them, but be sure and cover the pointy parts of the staple with duct tape.

Let the children enjoy hitting the balloon back and forth. Use a large space for this activity or do it outside. When doing this outside make it into a game by adding tape lines for boundaries. You can also put tape down the middle to create two sides and play the game like badminton. Children really enjoy hitting the balloons and even the timid enjoy it because it is soft and does not hurt if they get hit by the balloons.

Bubbles

It is fun to buy or make your own bubbles. Children love to blow and pop them. Do this activity outside. One child will blow the bubbles and the other child will pop them. Have them take turns being the blower and the popper. The teacher can also be the blower to one child at a time and have the child pop the bubbles following her/his directions. Examples of different ways to pop the bubbles would be - pop them with your foot, hand, or elbow.

Homemade Bubbles

Mix 2 cups water with 3 tablespoon liquid dish soap. Dawn original works best. Then, add 1/3 cup white corn syrup. Mix slowly. Place it in small containers for the children to use or you can double the ingredients to make larger amounts and place it into a pail with bubble blowers made from rounded wires with handles to create bubbles. You can also have children experiment with any toy that they can blow thought to make different shapes of bubbles.

FIELD TRIP IDEAS

You could arrange a trip to a barber shop. Children could see how they cut hair and see the tools that they use for shaving. Boys would really enjoy this. Ask the barber if the children could take a turn sitting in the special chair too.

As a follow up for the girls have a field trip to see a beauty shop. Ask the staff if the children can see the many things they do there besides cut hair like hair styling, permanent waves, and hair coloring. It would also be interesting for them to see how they give manicures and pedicures. Make sure that you have parents with you on these trips to help out. Also, take thank you cards that the children have made to give them when you arrive there.

Another great place to go is your local library. Be sure and plan this early so that you can be there for story time, finger play time and or puppet shows. Ask the staff to teach the children about book care while you are there. Make sure that the children have a special way of saying thanks.

One of the ways they can do this is by making a book using class drawings. The pictures can be placed in plastic sheet protectors and put into a small journal or punch holes in the papers so they fit the journal rings.

You can also make arrangements to go to Home Depot or Lowes. They do a good job at showing the children all the many things that they have for sale. The Home Depot also usually will have a craft for them to do there. The children love to do crafts and take them home to their family.

Like the other field trip places, you need to contact them early so that it will work with their schedule. Please also make sure you have parents with you and some special way of saying thanks.

Zoo Animals

🎵 MUSIC AND MOVEMENT

"Peek at a Peacock" from "I Have a Song For You About Animals" by Janeen Brady - Brite Music Enterprises, Inc.

"Monkey in the Treetop" from "I Have a Song For You About Animals" by Janeen Brady - Brite Music Enterprises, Inc.

"The Truth about Lions" from "I Have a Song For You About Animals" by Janeen Brady - Brite Music Enterprises, Inc.

"The Zebra" from "I Have a Song For You About Animals" by Janeen Brady - Brite Music Enterprises, Inc.

"Kangaroo, Kangaroo" from "I Have a Song For You About Animals" by Janeen Brady - Brite Music Enterprises, Inc.

"I Thought It was a Kitten" from "I Have a Song For You About Animals" by Janeen Brady - Brite Music Enterprises, Inc.

"Your Neck's So Long" from "I Have a Song For You About Animals" by Janeen Brady - Brite Music Enterprises, Inc.

"The Great Ape" from "I Have a Song For You About Animals" by Janeen Brady - Brite Music Enterprises, Inc.

All the songs from Brite Music are fun to use and the author also has a book with ideas for each of the songs on the tape.

"Elephants Elephants Everywhere" from "Finger Plays" by The Story Teller, 1995.

"Five Little Monkeys" from "Finger Plays" by The Story Teller, 1995.

"Mr. Alligator" from "Finger Plays" by The Story Teller, 1995.

Along with the music, The Story Teller also sells flannel figures that go with the tapes. Children enjoy these finger plays a lot.

"Here Sits A Monkey" from "The Corner Grocery Store" by Raffi.

"Going to the Zoo" from "Singable Songs for the Very Young" by Raffi. This song is fun for children to sing and pictures help the children to learn it. After they have learned the chorus and tune help them make up additional verses and use pictures to illustrate them. Look at all the zebras galloping around. See the examples below. You could also have children do other actions that you come up with to the songs like swimming movements.

You can download the following Magical David songs for free off the internet.

"Zelda the Zebra" from "Singing With Friends A Musical Journey with Magical David."

"Kiki Kangaroo" from "Singing With Friends A Musical Journey with Magical David."

"One For the Animals" from "Singing With Friends A Musical Journey with Magical David."

"Melvin The Monkey" from "Making Music with Mother Goose" by Jane Kitson, 2001.

"Freda Flamingo" from "Making Music with Mother Goose" by Jane Kitson, 2001.

Jane Kitson is a national early childhood consultant, author and recording artist. Her songs are designed for children ages 2-7. Her songs are simple and easy to learn.

"Animal Action 1" from "Kids in Motion" by Steve Millang and Greg Sceisa.

"Animal Action 11" from "Kids in Motion" by Steve Millang and Greg Sceisa.

These two songs by Steve and Greg were designed for creative movement and children enjoy movement that lets them be creative.

"The Alligator Chant" from "Dr. Jean Sings Silly Songs" by Dr. Jean.

"Monkeys and the Alligator" from "Dr. Jean & Friends" by Jean Feldman.

"Elephant Song" from "Dr. Jean & Friends" by Jean Feldman 1998.

"Boa Constrictor" from "Peter, Paul and Mommy" by Peter, Paul and Mary.

"A Trip To The Zoo" from "Macmillian Sing & Learn Program" by Newbridge Communications, Inc. This song is fun to act out and the tape gives the children directions as it is played.

"My Animals" from "Macmillian Sing & Learn Program" by Newbridge Communications, Inc.

"Camouflage" from "Macmillian Sing & Learn Program" by Newbridge Communications, Inc.

"Magic Land" from "Macmillian Sing & Learn Program" by Newbridge Communications, Inc.

"I Can't Spell Hippopotamus" from "Sing Along, Clap Along with Johnny Richardson" by Johnny Richardson. You can create cards to go with this song on your computer. You can make some similar to mine by using software for your computer or use clip art books. Here is an example of cards I use.

"The Cool Bear Hunt" from "Dr. Jean Sings Silly Songs" by Dr. Jean. This is a new modern version of Going On A Bear Hunt. This song has the children doing actions of going on a bear hunt in a different fun way.

"One Elephant Went Out To Play." The tune is the same as "One Little Duck Went Out to Play."

ONE ELEPHANT WENT OUT TO PLAY

One elephant went out to play,

on a bright and sunny day.

He had such enormous fun

that he called on __(child's name)__ elephant

to come and play.

Two elephants went out to play,

on a bright and sunny day.

They had such enormous fun

that they called on _____elephant

to come and play

Continue with each child in the same way, but on the last child change last part to that they played till the sun went down and they all ran away.

Make a simple finger puppet for each child in the class. The puppet will be an elephant head with a round hole where the child will place their finger to be the elephants' trunk. See the example below. Children will stand up when their name is called and sit down when they all run away.

72

"Brown Bear, Brown Bear, What Do You See?" by Eric Carle/Bill Martin.

When singing this song make your own pictures of the different animals and place them on a sheet of card stock to help children with the words to the song. You can use pictures from animal magazines or clip art that is colored the color you want them to learn.

Use the same words from the book while singing, such as red bird, red bird what do you see. This song is fun to sing and helps children learn their colors.

"Color Hoedown" from "Macmillian Sing & Learn Program" by Newbridge Communications, Inc. This song has a cute dance to go along with it included with the song. Children wear one of these colors red, yellow or blue bear heads from a yarn necklace. The song tells the children wearing different colors to do things like step inside the circle and tap and clap. Children really enjoy this activity.

LANGUAGE AND LITERACY

Zoo-Looking by Mem Fox, Scholastic Inc., 1996.

Hug by Jez Alborough, Scholastic Inc., 2001.

Eyes on Nature Apes and Monkeys by John Grassy, Kidsbooks, Inc., 1997.

Baby Animals Learn by Pamela Chanko, Scholastic Inc., 1998.

Curious George Visits The Zoo by Margret and H. A. Rey, Scholastic Inc., 1987.

Brown Bear, Brown Bear, What Do You See? by Eric Carle, Henry Holt and Company, 1992.

Polar Bear, Polar Bear, What Do You Hear? by Eric Carle, Henry Holt and Company, 1991.

Biggest, Strongest, Fastest by Steve Jenkins, Scholastic Inc., 1996.

Is Your Mama a Llama? by Deborah Guarino, Scholastic Inc., 1989.

Arctic Babies by Kathy Darling, Scholastic Inc., 1996.

The Amazing Panda Adventure by John Wilcox & Steven Alldredge, Scholastic Inc. 1995.

I Went to the Zoo by Rita Golden Gelman, Scholastic Inc., 1993.

Joey by Jack Kent, The Trumpet Club, 1992.

A Visit to the Sesame Street Zoo by Children's Television Workshop, Sesame Street Muppets, Random House/Children's Television Workshop.

Little Lions by Jim Arnosky, Troll, 1998.

Tilly and the Rhinoceros by Sheila White Samton, Philomel Books, 1993.

There's a Hole in My Pocket Adapted by Akimi Gibson, Scholastic Inc., 1994.

The Color Nature Library Baby Animals by Jane Burton, Crescent Books, 1978.

Good Night Gorilla by Peggy Rathmann, Scholastic Inc., 1995.

The Happy Lion by Louise Fatio, McGraw-Hill Book Company, A Children's Choice Book Club Edition by Macmillan Children's Book clubs.

Endangered Animals by Faith McNulty, Scholastic Inc., 1996.

Zoo Song by Barbara Bottner, Scholastic Inc.

The Baby Zoo by Bruce McMillan, Scholastic Inc., 1992.

Crocodile Smile by Sarah Weeks, Scholastic Inc., 1997. There is also a tape available for this book with 10 songs by Scholastic Inc.

Over in the Grasslands by Anna Wilson and Alison Bartlett, Scholastic Inc., 2001. There is also a tape of this book by Scholastic Inc. Children really enjoy this one.

Snap! by Marcia Vaughan, Scholastic Inc., 1994. There is also available a tape of this book by Scholastic Inc.

That's Good! That's Bad! by Margery Cuyler, Scholastic Inc., 1992. This is a funny book about what happens to a little boy while at the zoo. It has a companion tape by the same title from Scholastic Inc.

Rain by Manya Stojic, Scholastic Inc., 2000. This book tells what happens when it rains and the pictures show the animal's reaction in the wild to it. This book and accompany tape is from Scholastic Inc.

I Don't Want to go to Bed! by Julie Sykes, Scholastic Inc., 1996. This book is about a baby tiger that went exploring when his mother told him it was time for bed. There are nice pictures of all the other animals he meets and a sweet ending. This book also has a tape to go with it by Scholastic Inc.

A good way to purchase your books is through the Scholastic Book Club. They are high quality and the children in your class will have the opportunity to buy them through the club too. Belonging to the club doesn't cost you any money. You only have to pay for the books that you order. You can find it on the internet at their website.

SMALL GROUP ACTIVITIES/TABLE TIMES

MATH & COGNITIVE

Elephant Count

Use die cuts to punch out gray elephants or draw an outline of one and trace it onto gray paper. Use the drawing as a tracer to make sets of ten elephants for each child in your small group. Then use small sticker dots to place dots on the elephants. Place numbers 1-10 on the other side of the elephants making sure that the numbers correspond with the numbers written.

Start out by showing the children an animal card set. Hold each card up and have the children take turns counting the dots on the card. Then turn the card over and show the numeral for that amount of dots. Continue with each card until they have gone through all the cards in the set. If this unit is used at the first of the year only use the numbers 1-5. Then have the children pair up to use their own set to count dots and check what the number looks like on the other side. This way they can help each other. Later as the children feel comfortable using the numeral sets have them work with a partner to learn numeral names. They will also be doing the activity in a new way. Have them start with the elephants on the number side first and say the numeral name. Then they will check the dots on the other side to see if they named the numeral correct. As the children increase their knowledge of numbers have them use the rest of the set from 6-10 and proceed as before with the dot side first.

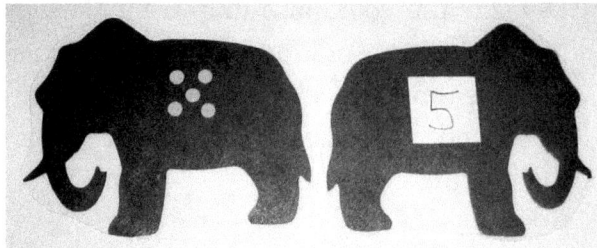

Zoo Leg Counting

This activity is a good one to start with when the children have had a little experience with numbers or counting. Cut out various zoo animals with different amounts of legs. An example would be a rhinoceros with four legs and a penguin with two legs. Place lots of animals on a poster board and include lots of different animals. Have the children take turns placing their finger on the legs of an animal and count them. Do this activity every day while you are talking about zoo animals.

Kangaroo Match

Use die cuts to punch out kangaroo shapes or draw an outline of one and trace it onto paper.

Using the drawing as a tracer, make a set for each of the shapes you would like the children to learn. Examples of different shapes are circle, square, triangle, diamond, heart, star, rectangle, and a crescent. Then make a smaller head and the top part of a baby of a kangaroo to represent a baby kangaroo. Then cut a small slit in the larger mother kangaroo for her pouch. Cut out a large and small kangaroo for each shape. Next make small shapes using colored construction paper and make them fit onto the heads of the two kangaroos, mom and baby. Glue on the shapes. Make sets and laminate them.

Now you are prepared to start the game. Place the larger mom kangaroos on the table one at a time and have the children repeat the shape names with you. Then take turns giving the children a small baby kangaroo and ask them to name their shape. If they need help have everyone say the name of the shape together with the child. Now have the child match the small body with the matching shape on its mom. Help them place it into the slot of the pouch. Have the children continue by giving another child a small body and do the same process again. Be sure and give positive comments to the children as they try to learn these new shape names.

Monkey Sizes

Find a picture of a monkey to use in this activity. I used a picture from Carson-Dellosa Publications number CD-5522. You could also draw a monkey, punch one out with a die cut machine or find a picture in a book or magazine. Then use a copy machine to decrease and/or increase its size three times, making a total of four different sizes. Make the sizes look clearly bigger and or smaller than the other pictures. Mount them or laminate them. Make two set of these monkeys.

In this activity, it is best to work with one child at a time. If it is the child's first experience finding big and little use only the biggest and littlest monkeys. Have the child point to the biggest and then the littlest monkey. When they can do that mix up the shapes and pick up one of the monkeys and have the child tell you the size of the monkey. Now pick up the other size and have the child tell you the size of it. Continue working with the child another day on the sizes and words used for the two sizes.

When the individual child has mastered that activity, introduce the middle size money along with the big and little monkey. Now do the activity like before by having the child point to the different sizes you say. Then mix them up and have the child say the size names for all three of the monkeys. Now have the child try to put them in order from smallest to largest. If the child can do that correctly, then have them learn terms like this is the small one and this is the middle sized one and this is the large one. Now mix them up and have the child put them in order and say the size names to you. When the child is able to say the sizes in comparison sizes and arrange them correctly add the last middle size monkey and proceed as before. Remember to take each step slowly so that the child has time to master the new terms and order.

Counting Animals

Buy a small set of zoo animals. They can often be purchased at a dollar store or at a school supply store. Work with children one at a time. First place five animals on the table all together. Have the child count them for you. If they need help, have the child slide each animal as they count them from one place across the table from the other animals and say one with the child. Then have the child slide another one across and say two with them. Continue until you have both counted to five. Wait for the next day and count in the same method again. Keep trying to help the child until they are able to complete the task, but don't do it over and over on one day. When the child says any of the numbers correctly, give them a smile and say, "I knew that you could do it!" or some other positive comment. Move on with counting to ten when the child has mastered 1-5.

Peanut Estimation

Provide a small glass container such as a clear, clean jam bottle. Also buy and place 5 peanuts that are in the shell inside the jar. Have the children make guesses (estimations) of how many peanuts are in the container. Write the child's name and the number that they guessed on a piece of paper.

Then let one of the children dump out the peanuts and have all the children count together to see how many there are. Then look at the paper to see who got close to that number. Now have them close their eyes while you put a different amount into the jar. Then have them open their eyes and make guesses again. Write down their new guesses and count how many there are this time. Next have a different child dump them out and count them to see who was close this time. Play continues while they are still interested.

Another day, play the game again. This time you will let the children take turns placing the peanuts in the jar while the others have their eyes closed. Select the amount of peanuts to have available for the children to use ahead of time. Note if any of the children have nut allergies and don't have nuts in the class room. You can still play the game, but choose other items to count that are of a large size like teddy bear crackers. You could also give children a treat of whatever you place in the jar for them after the activity has been completed.

FINE MOTOR SKILLS

Zebra Stripes

Draw a large outline of a zebra. Then cut the outline out and place it on top of five sheets of long black construction paper. Now trace around the shape with chalk and staple the sides of the papers together. Next, cut through the layers of paper to create five zebras. Continue tracing and cutting until you have reached the number needed for your class. Obtain books or pictures of zebras for the table so children can see what their stripes look like. Children will use chalk on the black paper to draw stripes on to their zebra.

Be sure and tell them to take their time to get the stripes the way that they want them to look.

Elephant Head

Give each child a sheet of gray construction paper to make an elephant head. Help them fold and crease the paper into thirds going across the width of the paper. Next with the paper still folded have them cut from bottom along both sides a diagonal line or you can place a card stock triangle for them to trace at the bottom of the fold so they can trace the diagonal line and cut along it. Now open up the folds and cut off a small triangle at the opposite end through a single thickness on both sides. This finishes the ears and creates the trunk. Provide markers or crayons for them to draw a face on their elephant.

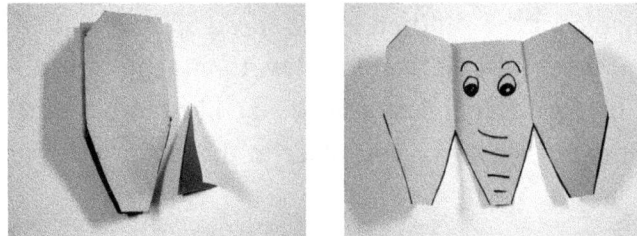

Camel Sponge Paint

Draw an outline of a camel or use a die cut and enlarge it on a copy machine to the size of your liking. Now place the large camel onto a sheet of heavy card stock and trace around it. Do this on several sheets so that more than one child at a time can do the activity. After it has been traced cut out the center shape by using an X-acto knife. This will create a stencil. Then apply clear wide tape around the edges of the stencil. This will enable the tape used to come off easily so that it can be used again. Place the camel stencil over a plain piece of paper and tape the edges of the stencil to the paper. Mix poster paints in a variety of colors by adding a little hand dishing soap to the paint. Put the paint on foam plates. Have the children use a square cut from a piece of a sponge to dip into the paint and then press onto their paper. Have the children wear paint aprons while doing this project. After the stencil has been filled in with color help the children carefully remove the stencil so another child can use it. Be sure that each child has their name written on their picture.

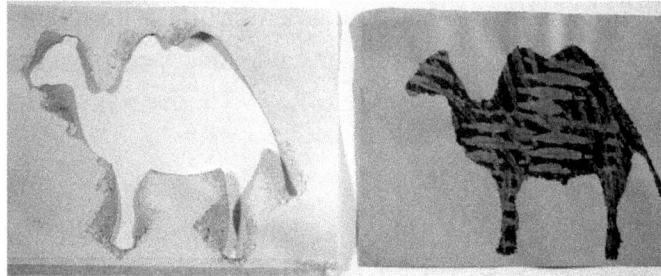

Lion Head

Provide paper plates, markers, crayons, googly eyes, small glue bottles, scissors, colored yarn and various colors of crepe paper for children to use for this project. Show the children pictures of male lions and point out their manes. Tell children that they will make lion heads using the various materials on the table. Tell them they can cut yarn or crepe paper to make manes for their lion or they can draw manes using the markers or crayons. Tell them to use a plate for the lion's head. Then let them make decisions on how to design their lion head.

Giraffe Head

Draw a long neck with a giraffe head on a piece of paper and make copies of it for each child. Have markers, crayons and black, dark gold and brown half sheets of paper with child size scissors and glue for the children to use. Show pictures of giraffes and tell the children to add details to their outline by adding eyes, mouth, nose spots and color to their giraffes.

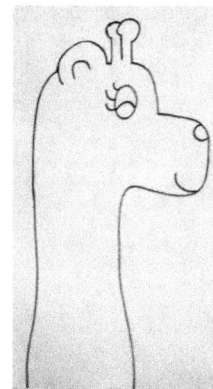

Zoo Hat

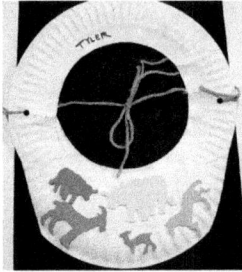

Provide paper plates, yarn, scissors, glue, small foam animal shapes and paper punches. Have the children fold a paper plate in half and cut a half circle out of the center of it. Then have them open up the fold and punch a hole on one side. Next have them punch another hole across from the first hole. Tie their yarn through the punched holes for them.

Have the children fold another plate in half and cut it along the fold line. One piece of it will be discarded and the other half will be the bill for the hat. Tape or staple the bill on the hat and trim the edge of the bill. Let the children collage foam animal shapes onto their hat with glue. Once the glue has dried, their hats can be tied under their chin for them to wear.

Alligator Cutting

Trace an alligator pattern in a line across the top of a page like in the example. Then, using a ruler, draw a straight line from the top line on the far left side of the paper. Then draw a curved line freehand about an inch from the first line. Now draw a straight line down the middle of the area and a zig zag line next to it. Finish up by drawing another curving line. Next add an alligator on the first line and on the middle line. If you need help drawing the alligators, find the shapes in a clip art book or have a friend help you. Copy the page onto green card stock paper so that it will be easier to cut. Children will each get a page to cut. This is a great page to help those who are just staring to use scissors or those that are still mastering the process.

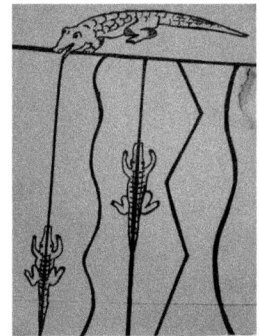

Monkey Tree

Have children trace and cut a pattern of a tree top and a tree trunk on colored construction paper. Then have them glue the tree to a piece of construction paper. Now have a child safe ink pad for them to ink their finger on. The end flat part of their index finger works best. They can do five little monkeys like the song or as many as they want. Next let them use a marker to draw legs, arms, a head, ears and faces on each of them.

Alligator Picture

Before you begin, make a pattern for an alligator such as the one in the example and copy it on dark green paper. Also mix 2 parts shaving cream with 1 part glue and enough coloring to represent the color of water you would like. Place the mixture in small foam bowls for two children to share.

Give each child their own alligator. Have the children cut it out and draw eyes mouth and teeth on it. Next have them put on aprons to protect their clothes. Now give each child a piece of cardboard and a craft stick. They will need to place their name on the back of the cardboard before beginning this project. Next have them use their sticks to scoop and spread the mixture over their board to represent water. When they have finished arranging it they will place their cut alligator on the water where they would like it. When it is dry hang them up with tacks or add a piece of yarn with the ends taped to the back of the cardboard, so they can be hung like a picture frame. The picture will have dimension.

LANGUAGE AND LITERACY

Zoo Cages

In this small group the teacher will prepare ahead of time colored construction paper. The papers will have holes punched along the top and bottom of the paper so that the punches are straight across from each other. If you would like the children to do this part, have a model for them to copy. You can also use a parent to help with this part. The teacher will also have yarn available for the children to thread through the punches to form the bars after the drawing are completed.

Children will be asked to draw a picture of their favorite zoo animal with markers or crayons. When they have completed their drawing they will tell the teacher the name of the animal and anything that they know about that animal that makes that animal special to them. The teacher and or helper will record their words on a piece of paper to be placed by their zoo car.

Animal Patterning Cards

Cut out squares in three different colors. Make five squares of each color. You will also need to purchase small zoo animal stickers. Place the same sticker animal on the same color of colored square, so that it will be easier for the children to make patterns. Now cover them with clear wide tape for durability and to be able to clean them.

Work with one or two children at a time. Show them how to make a two color pattern. Then have them take a turn adding a square to your pattern to have it continue correctly. Then have them take more turns until the colored squares have been used up. Now use one color that was the same one as before and the other color a new one. Have the children make a two color pattern again and only help when needed. If they were able to do this go on to the next step. If they were not quite ready go back to it another day.

When they are able to understand a two color pattern have them make a three color pattern. Have them help add colors to the pattern by taking turns as before. Remind then to look at the first part that you made to see what the color order was. After completing this pattern mix the squares up and have them make a different order using the three colors. Play continues one or two more times and then put it away for another day.

Eric Carle's 1,2,3 to the Zoo Matching Card Game by Scholastic

(Or another card matching game you buy from a children's toy store)

Place the cards face down on the table. The 1st player turns over three cards and names the animals or other picture. If two of them match, the player keeps the two that match and turns the other card back face down. If the cards didn't have a match place them all back face down. The 2nd player turns three cards over and looks for matches and proceeds as before. Be sure and have the children name the picture on each of the cards when they turn them over. If they need help, say the name and have the child repeat the name. Children should try to remember where the cards are on the table. Don't use the full deck at first because it will be too many for them to remember. Only have two or three children play at a time so that it doesn't take too long to play the game. Later when children are able to concentrate better, add more pairs to the game and another child may play too. You can also have the children say something more than the name of the animal or picture. Try words like what are the colors on that card or tell me something about that animal or picture.

What's Missing Game

Buy small plastic zoo animals to use for this game. Work with no more than two children at a time for this activity. Have the children sit across from you. Take one animal out at a time and ask the children the name of the animal. Have them help each other say the animal names. Only use the common animals because other unusual animals will be too hard for them. An example of some of the animals to use would be - lion, monkey, giraffe, zebra and alligator. Now line up three of the animals. Name them one more time and have the children say the names with you. Have the children cover their eyes. Take one of the animals away. Have the children uncover their eyes and look at the two remaining animals. Next say, "Which animal is missing?" Have them take turns answering the question. Put the animal back and play again. As the children learn the game add more animals to the line one at a time, so that it isn't too hard for them.

Animal Order Game

After learning the "What's Missing Game" have the children learn this new game. You will use the same plastic animals. Show them how to play the game by placing three animals in a straight line on the table in front of them. Then mix the order of the animals up and have them take turns putting them back in the order that they were in before you mixed them up. Do this a few times until they understand how to do it. Next tell the children that this time they need to look carefully at the order of the animals because this time they will have their eyes closed when you mix them up. Then have the children close their eyes and place a paper in front of the animals so that they can't peek and mix up the order of the animals. Tell them to open their eyes. Have one child arrange them back in the correct order. Tell the other children not to help this time and that it will be their turn next time. If the child gets mixed up it's ok. Don't comment, simply place them back in the correct order and give the next child their turn proceeding the same way as before. If the child gets it correct, say that they look the same and now it's another child's turn. Play this a few times and then return to it another day. When they are ready, add a fourth animal to the group. Play as before. The children love this game and it helps them learn the names of the animals and to recall information.

What's That Animal?

Purchase or find large photographs of zoo animals. Then place a piece of construction paper over the photo and note on the construction paper places that will show parts of the animal. Draw circles or other shapes where noted and cut around the shapes except leaving a small part to keep the shape attached to the rest of the paper. This will form small windows that can be opened or closed to reveal parts of the photo beneath it. Continue to do this with the other photos that you acquired.

Have a small group of children sit by you and tell the children that they are going to play a game called "What's That Animal." Show the first photo that has been covered by the paper and open one of the windows. Ask a child if he/she can tell what animal it is. If the child doesn't know, then open another window and have them guess what it might be. You may need to open another window. If the child still doesn't know ask others in the small group to tell what animal it is. Next take the paper off the photo and show it. Ask if they were correct with their guess or if they need help naming the animal. Then ask the children to tell you anything that they might know about the animal shown. Continue with the next photos one at a time as you did before. They really enjoy guessing the animals. When they get them correct before the whole photo has been shown, ask them how they knew that it was that animal.

Sound Game

Have a tape-recorder available with a blank tape for this game. Children will choose a zoo animal that they like during the day. Then later take turns having all the children go with you to a quiet place. Record the child saying the name of the animal and the sound it makes. An example would be - "I like lions, roaring sound." Make a list of the order that you record the children. Now you are ready to have the children in a small group listen to the tape and guess which child made the sound of each animal. Talk about listening to others and the importance of listening.

FREE TIME

CREATIVE ARTS

Play Dough

Prepare play dough for the children to create their own zoo animals. Provide craft sticks, rollers, texture plates and foam plates for the children to place their animals. Explain to the children that this is a special play dough that will be left to dry and that when it has dried they can paint their animals with poster paint or water colors. Provide pictures of zoo animals for the children to look at while creating their own animal. Make sure that their name is on their paper plate.

<u>Self- Hardening Play Dough Animals</u>

4 cups flour
1 ½ cups salt
1 tsp. alum
Optional 1-2 Tbs. food coloring

Mix the flour, salt and alum together. Then add the water to it gradually. *If you want the mixture colored, add the coloring to the water before stirring it into the flour. This will make the color smooth. Stir to form a ball in the bowl. Add more water if it won't hold together. Next, knead dough. Place in a sealed container until you are ready to use it. After shapes have been made leave them out to dry.

Finger Painting

Make chocolate and lemon pudding for this activity. Also have large sheets of paper and shapes of bears and giraffes for the children to choose what they would like to finger paint on. Make sure that they wash their hands and have an apron on before they start this activity. Children will use a small plastic spoon to add the pudding to their paper. Let them add either color of pudding or some of both to their paper to move around with their fingers and create curves and waves. It's okay if they lick their fingers, since they washed them first. Monitor the amount of pudding placed on their paper, so no one gets way too much.

Easel Painting

Either mix poster paints in different colors or put out water colors for children to paint with. Encourage them to paint animals or birds. Place plain large sheets out for them to paint on, as well as shapes of bears, giraffes, parrots and or tigers. Let them choose which shape they want and what colors to use.

Sock Puppet

For this project collect good socks from parents. Large socks that are missing their mate work great. If not, buy socks that are on sale in bright colors or buy cheap ones at dollar store. Then collect various items for the children to use to create their own zoo animal sock puppet. Some examples of materials to collect would be - feathers, large colored foam squares, wiggly eyes, buttons, colored cotton balls, small pom poms, colored yarn, colored pipe cleaners, material scraps, markers, scissors, and glue. Let the children choose their sock and place a stiff piece of paper inside the sock, so the glue doesn't glue the sock together. Then let them use the materials to create their own sock puppet zoo animal.

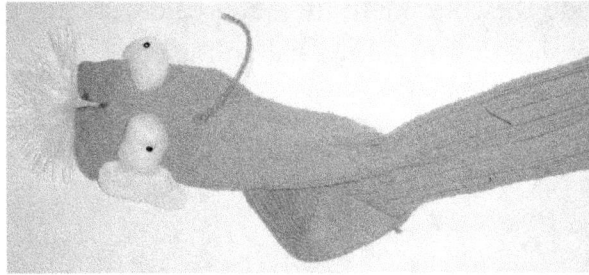

SENSORY

Sand

Fill a tub or sensory table with sand and provide twigs with small leaves, craft sticks, rocks and other items for the children to create an interesting place for the zoo animals to live. Also place plastic zoo animals for the children to play with.

Soil

Use potting soil or plain dirt for the children in tubs or at the sensory table. Children can go outside with you to find items to add to the soil to make it seem more like where animals might live. Take a pail for this and encourage them to be creative. When you go inside with the items ask the children to vote which items they would like to use and talk about how to use the items brought inside before placing them in the soil. Next have them decide which plastic animals to add to the project. Encourage them to make things to go in the tub. If this project goes well you could provide shoe boxes for the children to create their own zoo or jungle. Let them make props and decide ahead of time how many plastic animals they may keep for the project.

DRAMATIC PLAY & SOCIAL DEVELOPMENT

Zoo

Children can pretend to have their own zoo by providing many stuffed animals and cardboard boxes for cages. Also provide a cash register and papers cut for tickets for entrance into the zoo. There can also be tags for tour guides to wear and counters set up for buying food. Children can wait on the people coming to the zoo and give out plastic foods for them to eat. They can also have someone be an animal trainer and have a performance with children wearing animal costumes. Teachers can ask for parents to donate or loan them Halloween costumes of animals or try to purchase them at thrift store.

Jungle

Use stuffed animals and costumes as in the zoo play, but also use a small tent for camping in the jungle along with camping equipment like sleeping bags. Other things to have on hand would be pans, pots, pretend foods, binoculars, hunting or camouflage clothing and hats. You could also have children make their own binoculars by taping two empty tubs together and punching a hole in each side to string a piece of yarn through and tie it to the other side to form a loop so they can hang them around their neck.

Another item they can make with your help would be a hunting vest made from a large paper grocery sack. Directions for the vest are: Take a large grocery bag and with the bottom flap against the bag body cut a "v" shape in the middle going through both thicknesses. This will become the top of the vest and where heads will go. Then open the sides of the bag and close to the bottom flap near the "v" shape cut a 6 inch circle out for an arm hole. Now turn the bag to the other side and do the same thing for the other arm hole. This will be put on like a T-shirt. The children can decorate them with different colors of small pieces of crepe paper and cut construction paper that they glue onto the front and back. This will help the vest look like camouflage.

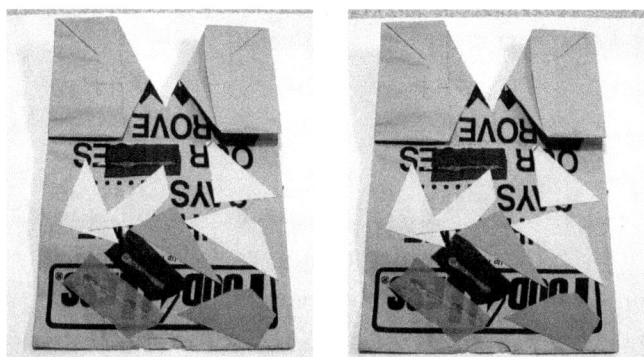

SCIENCE

Make small signs saying fur, skin and feathers. Place different feathers by the one saying feathers and fur by the fur one and leather or vinyl by the skin one. If you have access to types of skin such as alligator or snake skin place it with the skin sign also. Then place books on the table with zoo animals that have features that have feathers, fur and skin. Also provide a magnifying glass close by for children to use. Children can now explore the items on the table. See the example below.

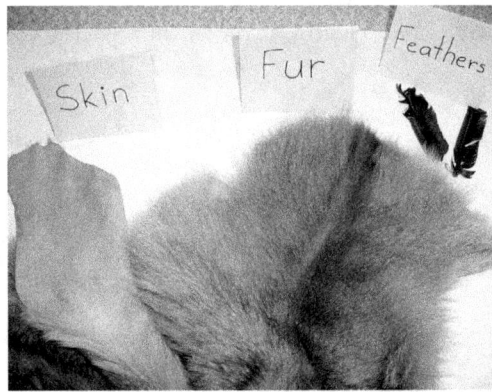

Another idea for the table would be to use a small box such as a shoe box and cut a small hole into the center section of the lid. Then put feathers, fur, tree bark, pom poms, small pieces of sand paper and pieces of leather or vinyl in the box. Cover the lip of the box using a piece of material that has been taped on to the lid on one side. Tell the children to put their hand inside and find one object at a time to feel without looking inside. Then ask them to tell you about the things they felt. You can help make them more aware of the things by asking questions such as, "How did that item feel when you touched it?" or "What other items felt the same way as that one did?"

GROSS MOTOR SKILLS

Zoo Hokey-Pokey

Children will sing and move like different zoo animals while doing the "Hokey-Pokey." Show the children how this is done by choosing an animal and then singing the words and doing the movements like this animal would. For example you might want to be a bear. You would sing, "You shake your bear paws in and you shake your bear paws out, you do the zoo pokey and you turn yourself about." After showing the children let them choose a zoo animal and show the class what to do and then have the class sing and do the movements with the child.

Five Little Monkeys Jumping On a Bed

Sing the song "Five Little Monkeys Jumping on a Bed" and instead of doing finger play actions, have the children stand up and pretend to be jumping up and down on a bed. Have them get down on the floor to pretend to roll off the bed. You can do this activity all together or five children at a time and use a real blanket to roll off.

Animal Walks

Have the children pretend to be different animals like a lion or a snake and move from one area to another doing the movement like that animal. For example, you could be a snake and lie down on the floor and slither around.

Bean Bag Toss

Acquire a large box and draw simple outlines of animals on the four sides of the box. Draw extra large mouths on the animals. Then cut out the mouth area and a little of the body too. Make sure the opening is larger than 12 inches square. If this project is too much for you just make lines for the area that you want them to hit with a bean bag instead of cutting it out.

Have the children stand about three feet from the box on all four sides of the box. Give instructions of when to throw a bean bag before you give them one to hold. Tell them to aim and throw the bean bag at the animal's mouth after you and the children chant together the name of the animal.

Animal Relay

Supply a stuffed animal for each group of 5-7 children. Have the children line up in straight lines. If you have lots of children in your class make more lines of children. Explain how to play the game and give each team a stuffed zoo animal. Tell the children to start the race when you say, "Go, go zoo animals."

To play the game, children will pass the animal over their head to the person behind them. Then the next person will pass it behind them and so on until it reaches the last child who will run up to the front of their line and pass it this time between their legs to the person behind. They will continue to pass it back between their legs until they reach the last person again. Then that last person will take the animal to the front and everyone on that team will sit down. All the children will do the same activity in their lines. Each line will try and race to be the fastest team to be able to sit down.

FIELD TRIP IDEAS

This would be a great time to have parents go with you to the zoo for the day. Have the children assigned in small groups with a teacher or parent. Have a meeting place for lunch and a time to be there. It's fun to take your lunches and eat together. It's also a good idea to have the same color T- shirts on the children to help spot them and keep them close to each other. Don't put names on them for safety sake, but put the name of your school and a phone number that could be your cell phone or someone else that could help if something goes wrong.

Talk with parents and children about learning and recognizing the animals that you have been talking about at school. Have them observe those animals first. Make sure the parents know which animals they have been learning about. If there is a children's zoo be sure and have them visit there and have a chance to pet the animals. Don't stay too long so that the children don't get too tired. Have a time and a place to meet at the end of the day. Ask parents to bring their cell phones if possible so that you can communicate with each other.

If you are unable to go to the zoo, contact a university that might let you come to their zoology department. They might have animals there for the children to see, touch and learn about. Often they have snakes, lizards and other animals or they might have stuffed animals to see.

There might also be places that might have bison, camels or llama to see. They have become more popular in the country and can be found in similar places that you find sheep.

Where To Get What You Need

There are many different places to get what you need. If you use your imagination, many items can be substituted for what you have on hand, can get for free, etc. For example, you may have an abundance of baby food jars from a family toddler. You can easily convert these to be part of a project. Teaching is also about being resourceful. Have family, friends, students and yourself save:

- Baby food jars

- Toilet paper rolls

- Paper towel rolls

- Scraps of material

- Extra tile

- Extra pieces from home improvement projects

- Coffee cans

- Oatmeal containers

- 2 liter bottles

- Cereal boxes

- Egg carton

- Milk jugs

- Salt containers

- Anything you can think of to be re-purposed for a learning tool

Other places to get materials include:

- Home improvement stores (Lowes or Home Depot)

- Dollar Stores

- Educational Supply Stores

- Grocery Store

- Party Supply Store

- Online Resources:

  — Oriental Trading Company: www.orientaltrading.com

  — http://www.etacuisenaire.com

  — Many great songs and activities are available from http://www.newbridgeonline. com/, which is where you can find the MacMillan Sing and Learn songs and other activities. Use the search function and type in "songs for learning". You may also be able to find these used online at www.alibris.com, www.amazon. com, or www.abebooks.com.